W9-BCP-787

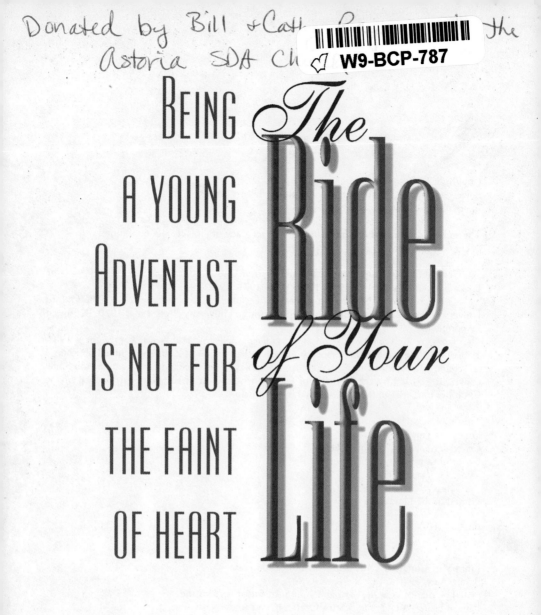

BEING *The* A YOUNG ADVENTIST *Ride* IS NOT FOR *of Your* THE FAINT *Life* OF HEART

ALEX BRYAN   VICTOR CZERKASIJ   ANDY NASH

REVIEW AND HERALD® PUBLISHING ASSOCIATION
HAGERSTOWN, MD 21740

The authors assume full responsibility for the accuracy of all facts and quotations
as cited in this book.

Scripture quotations marked NASB are from the *New American Standard Bible,* © The
Lockman Foundation 1960, 1962, 1963, 1968, 1971, 1972, 1973, 1975, 1977.

Texts credited to NEB are from *The New English Bible.* © The Delegates of the Oxford
University Press and the Syndics of the Cambridge University Press 1961, 1970. Reprinted
by permission.

Texts credited to NIV are from the *Holy Bible, New International Version.* Copyright © 1973,
1978, 1984, International Bible Society. Used by permission of Zondervan Bible Publishers.

Bible texts credited to NRSV are from the New Revised Standard Version of the Bible,
copyright © 1989 by the Division of Christian Education of the National Council of the
Churches of Christ in the U.S.A. Used by permission.

This book was
Edited by Tim Lale
Cover designed by Matthew Pierce
Cover illustration by Art Landerman
Type: 11.5/13.5 Weiss

Printed in the U.S.A.

00 99 98 97 96   5 4 3 2 1

Library of Congress Cataloging in Publication Data
Bryan, Alex, 1970-
    The ride of your life : being a young Adventist isn't for the
faint of heart / Alex Bryan, Victor Czerkasij, and Andy Nash.
          p.   cm.
    Summary: Uses a Seventh-day Adventist perspective to discuss the
Christian life as a journey filled with joy and challenges.
    1. Teenagers—Religious life.   2. Seventh-day Adventists—
Membership—Juvenile literature.   [1. Seventh-day Adventists.
2. Christian life.]   I. Czerkasij, Victor.   II. Nash, Andy, 1971-
III. Title.
BX6184.B78   1996   96-46654
248.8'3—dc21   CIP
                                                       AC

ISBN 0-8280-1066-8

DEDICATION

"To those
   —family, friends, teachers, pastors
   —who kindle and shape our hope
       in Jesus Christ and in His church.

"His divine power has given us everything we need for life and godliness through our knowledge of him who called us by his own glory and goodness. Through these he has given us his very great and precious promises, so that through them you may participate in the divine nature and escape the corruption in the world caused by evil desires."
                              —2 Peter 1:3, 4, NIV.

Contents

"For if you possess these qualities in increasing measure, they will keep you from being ineffective and unproductive in your knowledge of our Lord Jesus Christ."

—*2 Peter* 1:5-8.

Introduction

FEELING A LITTLE FAINT

A n d y   N a s h

"'Hear, O Israel, today you are going into battle against your enemies. Do not be fainthearted or afraid; do not be terrified or give way to panic before them'" (Deuteronomy 20:3, NIV).

I've never been real big into farm animals. I like milk, but I don't care to watch where it comes from. I prefer three-wheelers over horses—three-wheelers don't go berserk when they catch sight of the barn. And though I've heard many times that pigs are smart, I've never bothered to find out what they're smart at.

Nevertheless, a newspaper article about some high-strung goats in St. Cloud, Florida, recently piqued my interest. This rare breed of goats will faint when they get excited. The goats suffer from a genetic disorder that locks up their muscles at the slightest disturbance. To onlookers, the goats appear to faint.

Cool, I thought. *Fainting goats.* This I had to see.

Since St. Cloud lies just south of my Orlando home, I decided to call the goat breeders, Danny and Lois Hall, and ask them to let me see their fainting goats.

"Sure," Lois Hall said. "Come on out and see them for yourself."

Two hours later Lois and I were bumping along on a loader through the pasture. "There's two of them over there," said Lois, pointing. Sure enough—two normal-looking goats grazed peacefully 50 yards ahead of us. At 30 yards one of the fainting goats jerked his head up. At 20, they tried to run away. At 15, they keeled over.

"When they're afraid, they faint," Lois said, shaking her head. "It's kind of amazing."

Lois says her goats faint all the time: when they try to climb the food trough and get scared; when someone or something, such as a cow, sneaks up on them; even when someone's just being friendly.

Kathy Heiken, a breeder in Des Moines, can vouch for that. "I walked up to the fence one day and said, 'Hi, kids. How are you doing?' and two fainted."

Another breeder, Pat Moore in Nixa, Missouri, reports a 1990 mass fainting involving 75 goats, an auction tent, and the wind. When the tents snapped, the goats dropped. "All but two pens of them just went down, like on cue," says Pat.

The goats remain down for about 20 seconds, says Ruth Prentice of the International Fainting Goat Association. "Then," she says, "they'll get back up and drag their hindquarters for another 10 to 15 seconds until their muscles loosen up."

Only two thousand legitimate fainting goats live in the United States, and they bring from $200 to $500 apiece. To register a fainting goat, the owner must show a picture of the goat in the process of fainting.

Quite a life these goats live, isn't it? They wake up in the morning and spend the day feeling threatened and falling down. It doesn't take much to shock them. A greeting, a breeze, the sight of their friends fainting. Anything unexpected, any change in their little lives, and they're gone. Poor things. They're as high-strung as some young Adventists I know.

Yes, *young* Adventists. Not long ago these amazing fainting goats would have reminded me of the older generations of Adventists. After all, who would panic if a young woman wore a short skirt to church? Who would lock up if a special-music soundtrack had a beat? Who would keel over if the pastor and his family swam on Sabbath? The older Adventists, of course. But that's ancient history.

These days it's not the older generation that faints left and right. They're used to surprises by now. They've seen it all. No, it's us. The Adventist Baby Busters. We're the ones locking up and dropping over. We're the ones trying to establish our niche in the world, find our place in the church, and do both as smoothly as possible.

When that doesn't happen, we freak.

Becky, a student at an Adventist college, decides she wants to be a student missionary the year after she graduates. She reads about calls in Southeast Asia and sees one she likes—teaching English and Bible. She loves the Lord and can't wait to share His love with those who haven't heard about it. She mentions her plans to an Adventist professional in her field of study. "Boo!" The professional tells her that going overseas is a bad idea, that she'll have trouble breaking into the job market when she returns. Becky freezes. She decides not to go.

A young couple, Jared and Jenny, both grow up in the Adventist Church. They marry, move to a small northwestern town, join the local church, and make friends with other Adventist couples their age. Their new friends are different, though. They often poke fun at Adventist doctrine and lifestyle. They don't seem to enjoy the worship service half as much as they do complaining about it afterward. They don't hold, nor will they accept, any leadership positions in the church. They are too busy for that. Jared and Jenny are confused. They don't like their friends' attitude toward the church, but they don't like church without their friends. So they drop out altogether.

Phil, a young Adventist, can't believe what he's just heard. His favorite pastor ever—the one who preached with so much energy, the one who loved water sports, the one who baptized Phil's sister—has destroyed his own family. He has run off with a woman in the church, and two spouses and four children have been left behind. The pastor quits the ministry and marries the woman. Phil freezes. He still attends church, but halfheartedly. He wonders, *If I can't trust my favorite pastor, whom can I trust?*

Real stories. Real struggles. Maybe one of these is yours. Maybe you have your own variation. If you're young and Adventist and serious about it, you know the possible pitfalls. Like Becky, you know Adventism doesn't always line up well with the world. Like Jared and Jenny, you know how other "Adventists" can drag you down. Like Phil, you know what it's like to be disillusioned with someone who seemed to have it all together.

And we get disappointed.

That's nothing new. Disappointment laid the foundation of this church. The church's founders (many of whom were our age) staked their lives and reputations on an October arrival of Jesus. And when He didn't break through the clouds, a shaking set in.

"Forget this!" said hundreds of young Adventists (then Millerites). "We have better things to do with our time than get disappointed every few months."

One hundred and fifty years later, we're saying the same thing.

What to do? Remain right in the heart of an imperfect church that consistently lets us down? No way, we say. So many thousands of us either drop out or drift to a place where our lowered expectations will easily be met, out on the fringe. Makes sense, doesn't it? Risk less, lose less.

You know the story. Don't teach Sabbath school class, or you might be called a hypocrite. Don't support church standards, or your peers might consider you "uncool." Don't mention the name "Adventist" around work, or you might be associated with the Branch Davidians or the Mormons. And by all means, don't sit up front and center in church, or the church elders might try to visit with you and talk about the Lord's tender mercies and make you uncomfortable. Stay on the fringe, and church life will be easier. Right?

One other thing about those fainting goats. Legend has it that years ago sheepherders in the Tennessee hills would place these goats—they called them "scaregoats"—on the fringes of their flocks as a security measure—as a sacrifice. When a predator attacked, the goats would flinch, lock up, drop over, and provide an easy meal. And the sheep that stuck close to the shepherd could escape.

Here's the deal. If you're going to be an Adventist, be an active, committed, contributing Adventist. Ground yourself so strongly in the doctrines that you won't lock up when someone shreds them. Get so caught up in our message—Jesus *is* coming again—that nothing can keep you down. Lean into the curves, deal with the difficulties, rejoice in the truths—not for them, but *in* them. And above all, keep believing *wholeheartedly* that Jesus is in control and that He's led you to this church for a special purpose.

Because He has.

"For this very reason, make every effort to add to your faith . . ."

WILD RIDE
Alex Bryan

*A*ndy's favorite song is Michael Card's "Joy in the Journey." I should know. I lived next door to him in a college dormitory for a year. "Joy in the Journey" vibrated through his speakers—and my walls—more often than all other music combined (including the soothing melodies of Kenny G, which finished a distant second).

"Joy in the Journey" is not only Andy's favorite song; it's the way he views the Christian life—a journey filled with joy. And I agree. A walk with God is *joyous*. I also see the Christian life as a wild ride. A particular wild ride. Let me explain.

When I was 16, like many 16-year-olds, I became a licensed driver. The day I walked out of the DMV office holding my plastic card with a bad picture was the greatest day of my life—notwithstanding the day Michael Jordan sank a jump shot that gave the North Carolina Tar Heels the national college basketball championship.

As a 16-year-old, I knew a lot, of course. What I didn't know was how to drive (which I later discovered included many things). Three automobile accidents in the next 12 months proved this beyond doubt. One of the three I will never forget.

Driving home late one Friday night in my dad's car, I was appreciating some luxuries I could not enjoy in my 1977 Chevy Nova: heat, comfortable leather seats, and cruise control. That night the heat and the leather seats made me drowsy . . . unto sleep. Tragically, the cruise control did not sleep.

Cruising down the highway at 60, I began to dream about owning a car like this one day. Moments later total relaxation turned to complete panic. The sound of the car hurtling down into the median shocked the slumber out of me. I grabbed the wheel and cut back onto the road to the right. Too far. I cut back to the left. Way too far. I found myself across the median and into the oncoming traffic. As I cut back right across the median again, a tire blew. I kept lunging back and forth, trying desperately to control the automobile.

THE RIDE OF YOUR LIFE

Finally it hit me: *The cruise control is on!* I mashed the brake pedal. The car decelerated, and I pulled to the side of the road. The frame looked twisted. A wheel was trashed. I was suddenly in debt. But the wild ride was over.

I took a second wild ride more recently. Last summer, at age 24, I drove a van of teenagers to Charlotte, North Carolina, to spend a day at an amusement park. No, nothing wild happened on the way.

Some of the girls wanted me to try the newest roller coaster. We made our way through the gate to the place where we would board the roller coaster. I walked carefully, avoiding the expression of gastric discontent a previous roller-coaster rider had left behind—a warning for all who dared go any further that I did not heed.

The lady with the red shirt in the Plexiglas box waved us on board the roller coaster. The sign above warned that the elderly, people with bad backs, pregnant women, individuals with heart problems, and Alex Bryan should not ride the roller coaster. Ignoring the warning, I sat down in the plastic seat and pulled the black "safety" harness over my shoulders. A tone sounded. The roller coaster jerked to a start, and off we went.

Slowly we climbed up the first incline until we reached the top. Down, down, down, down, down, down we fell. And then my stomach came down too. We turned and twisted and flew upside down. We corkscrewed and sped up and slowed down. We jerked right and then left. Then we seemed to go right and left at the same time. We fell once more and finally came to a stop. And I didn't lose my breakfast! In fact, I wanted to go again.

If I invited you to jump into my car and take a ride and told you I'd drive like a maniac, roll the car, swerve all over the road, dodge other cars, and risk our lives every second, would you take me up on the offer? Probably not.

If I invited you to an amusement park and asked you to join me on the roller coaster, would you accept? The roller coaster would swerve and twist and turn and go upside down and everything. But you would still probably accept.

Why? The roller coaster runs on a track. It is designed to do all those crazy things. The person who built it knew how to make the ride wild and crazy and still make it safe. But I alone would be in control of my car.

Real Christianity is a thrilling ride, but Someone remains in control. Since the fall of this world Jesus has asked His people to be risk-takers, to live eventful lives filled with changes, new directions, and the unknown. He stands behind it all.

God asked Paul to change course completely from what he had spent his whole life fighting for. He asked Peter and Andrew and James and John to give up their lifelong occupations to become His evangelists. And He asked a rich ruler to give away all his wealth and power and become a child of God.

God asked Abraham to move his entire family and take up residence in a place he'd never seen. He asked Joseph to marry a pregnant girl. And He asked Moses to give up the highest position in Egypt—heir to the throne of the greatest superpower in his day—and spend the rest of his years in the desert: 40 of them alone, and 40 with a throng of unruly former slaves.

With God, every day is an unbelievable adventure. Adventist student missionaries have told me. Adventist evangelists in the former Soviet Union have told me. Adventist pastors, leading risk-taking churches for the cause of lost people in their communities, have told me. Adventists in my neighborhood have told me.

To those afraid of taking the wild ride of Christian discipleship I can offer no clever arguments. A compelling theological treatise would be useless. I offer the words of a roller-coaster Christian named Paul, who says: "Forgetting what is behind and straining toward what is ahead, I press on toward the goal" (Philippians 3:13, 14, NIV). "For I am convinced that neither death nor life, neither angels nor demons, neither the present nor the future, nor any powers, neither height nor depth, nor anything else in all creation, will be able to separate us from the love of God that is in Christ Jesus our Lord" (Romans 8:38, 39, NIV).

I can only offer you Jesus Christ: Jesus, who says, "I am with you always." Jesus, who wants you to experience the ride of your life. Jesus, who controls the ride. Jesus, who wants your wild ride to continue in heaven, forever.

"For this very reason, make every effort to add to your faith . . ."

MUSTARD SEEDS, PEACH PITS, AND BOWLING BALLS

Victor Czerkasij

My son Alex, who is 2½, loves to sit in a countertop chair for his meals. He likes it because Daddy sits in one just like his, and his chair is adjusted to make him eye level with me. I don't care for it much, because he can see my plate and whether or not I've finished my dessert. It's hard to resist a cute kid staring at you. And your dessert.

Lately Alex has begun to repeat a phrase that peppers most of his speech: *"By myself!"* He applies it to dressing and eating, and he once said it while sitting in the driver's seat of my car. I pointed out that he was 14 years too early.

The other evening, after a supper during which I didn't get much dessert, I leaned over to help Alex out of his countertop chair. "By myself!" he said. *All right*, I thought, and backed off.

He twisted around and began a slow slide toward the floor. He stretched and stretched, toes searching for solid ground. He was losing his grip.

I could see about an inch of space between Alex's foot and the floor. But he, slipping and whimpering, felt sure he was dangling miles above it and would hit the ground with a painful thud.

His shrieking persuaded me to let him gently down that last inch.

Some Seventh-day Adventists, like my son Alex, want to live by the phrase *by myself*. Though our unique heritage provides us with the assurance of God's leading in our denomination, and, figuratively speaking, we sit at the banquet table, some of us would like to slip out of the chair and leave the table.

"By myself," we insist, sure of our abilities and positive of success— until we find ourselves hanging, losing our grip, and wondering, *How could I have ended up like this? Where is my Father? Where is my faith?*

Until we reach the communion of heaven, God has given us the communion of one another, in our Seventh-day Adventist Church. It is here that the body grows to maturity with Him. If this model is ignored or disregarded, we end up like Alex—doubting and shrieking for help.

One of the curses facing God's people through history has been that great heights offer the opportunity for great falls. Sitting high means that the floor is just that much farther away. But "sitting high" in this church is no reason to worry. That's where we belong.

My coauthors, Andy and Alex, couldn't be more different from me and each other. They were born into this church; I was born far from it. Alex and I are pastors; Andy is assistant to the editor for the *Adventist Review*. Andy proposed to his wife with a multimedia production. I proposed to my wife in a parking lot. Alex proposes that one day he'll find a girl.

But we share a passion that right here, in this church family, we find new facets in the resurrected life of Jesus Christ. Here, in this church family, we first saw Him modeled and demonstrated. And, through His mercy, patience, and grace, we wish to reveal Him in these pages.

We don't pretend to have all the answers. We too wrestle with doubts. (The biggest one looks at me in the mirror every day!) You've heard before that claiming membership in the Seventh-day Adventist Church in no way guarantees that one has developed a strong faith in God. We still find ourselves asking, *"How can I really know faith? How can I be assured of all that He promises?"* But Jesus knows our battles with doubt.

For three years the disciples watched Jesus perform miracles and heard Him testify to being the Son of God. And yet Philip said, "Lord, show us the Father and that will be enough for us" (John 14:8, NIV). We would call this a serious body blow in physical terms, considering that Philip spoke *the Thursday evening before the Crucifixion.*

"Jesus answered, 'Don't you know me, Philip, even after I have been among you such a long time? Anyone who has seen me has seen the Father. How can you say, "Show us the Father"?' " (verse 9).

I sometimes make presentations about the college I work for. I like to think that when I finish, people will say, "Thanks. Now we know more about your college." If someone stood up and said, "Yes, this has all been quite entertaining, but when are you going to tell us about your college?" I would feel sad.

We can build faith one way only: *by living according to what we are already convinced is right.* Jesus marveled at the faith of those outside His specially chosen people. The Roman centurion and the Samaritan woman, for example. Their secret, it seems, was to live according to the light they had. Can you imagine what a change would happen if we all prayed for the courage to follow our convictions, as odd as they may sound to us or others?

God asks us not to believe through our ideas of logic or intellect, but merely *to believe*. To define successful faith, we need not measure it as the size of a mustard seed, a peach pit, or a bowling ball. No matter what its size, faith must be practiced in order for it to grow.

I recently heard about Eli Herring, a top lineman and draft pick in the NFL. ESPN reported that this young man has alerted teams that he won't play on Sunday, the day he believes is the Lord's rest day. He will trade $400,000 a year in pro football for $22,000 a year as a high school math teacher.

Of course, somebody in our church family might snort, "He doesn't even have the right day!" No, but he possesses the right spirit. And God will bless him with more truth at the right time because he lives according to his active conscience. Can we say the same?

And that's why Jesus felt hurt when Philip asked for more. The evidence for belief in God's promises, the Son of God Himself, had worked wonders in front of the disciple's face. No stronger testimony would come his way. Likewise, we will not receive better confirmation than the light we already have.

"Therefore, my brothers, be all the more eager to make your calling and election sure. *For if you do these things, you will never fall*" (2 Peter 1:10, NIV).

"For this very reason, make every effort to add to your faith . . ."

PHONE CALLS
Andy Nash

*T*he phone rings. I knew it would. I grab it.
"Hello, Dad?"
"Hi, pal."
"Well, who won?" I yell.
"Unbelievable," he says calmly.

He always has to build it up until I nearly go crazy. There I am, in Thailand in late October, waiting to hear how my favorite baseball team, the Minnesota Twins, has done in game 7 of the World Series against Atlanta, and my dad is prolonging the agony. I can hardly stand it.

"Unbelievable," he says again.
"Da-aad!"
"After nine innings, no score."
"No way!"
"Yes. Then Morris retired the side in the tenth."
"Yeah, and . . ."
"Larkin singled home the winning run."
"What, Dad? What? You mean, we—"
"World champs."

I've seen some good AT&T commercials over the years, but I think this call would have ranked right up there with the best. Father and son, 6,000 miles apart, sharing a great moment, bordering on the hysterical.

❊ ❊ ❊

The phone rings. I don't want it to. I know my voice will break.
"Hello."
"Hi, And. It's Angel."
"Oh, hi, Ange."
"Andy, what's wrong?"
"What do you mean?"
"Something's wrong. I can tell."

"Yeah, there is."

I'm home on my first break from college. Earlier I took our well-loved white Westie terrier, Casey, outside for a walk. She didn't want to come back in, so I let her stay outside. Soon after, someone came pounding at the front door. Next I was driving to the animal hospital. Fast. Then I was driving home. Slowly.

"Casey's dead, Angel."

"What?"

"I left her outside, and she got hit. The lady said Casey chased a squirrel right under her car."

"Are you sure she's dead?"

"I just went to see her at the vet."

My sister is crying. "Ange?"

"Pick me up."

I drive over to the academy and find Angel still by the phone booth. She climbs into my car. But we don't drive anywhere. We just hug and cry together for a few minutes. We have both lost a friend.

❀ ❀ ❀

The phone rings. I ignore it. Another ring. I roll over. The phone rings 200 more times. I decide to pick up.

"Hello?"

"Andy?"

"Yeah."

"I'm sorry. Were you asleep?"

"No. I was just getting up."

"You were asleep, weren't you?"

"Yeah."

"What time did you get back?"

"About 4:30, or something like that."

"Oh, poor thing. Are you exhausted?"

"I don't know. What time is it, anyway?"

It's almost noon, and I've been working the night shift at a Florida honeybee farm all week. My friends, the Emdes, need the help, and I need the work. My girlfriend, Cindy, is calling from Chattanooga just to brighten my spirits. As usual.

"So did you get stung?"

"No, not yet. I stopped eating honey last night, though. I thought I would never get tired of it, but I am now."

She's laughing.

"Well, if I were down there, I'd bring you a little snack around midnight."

"I know, but then you'd catch me with my honey."

"Oh, stop."

"OK, I'm sorry. I borrowed that one, anyway. So what have I done to deserve a long-distance call from you?"

Nothing. And that's the point. No big reason to chat—just for the fun of it.

And so go our lives—filled with calls of joy, grief, and plain silliness from those we love. It's usually nice to receive them. Talking to each other draws us closer.

And we can't help wondering, *Why doesn't God do this too?* Why doesn't He ever "call" to share exciting news or to cry with us or just to chat? Doesn't He know how nice it would be to hear His soothing voice—especially when we're hurting? We call Him all the time. Why doesn't He ever call us?

After all, God seemed to be calling people in Bible times. "So God said to Noah . . ." (Genesis 6:13, NIV). "Then God said to Abraham . . ." (Genesis 17:9, NIV). "And God spoke to Israel . . ." (Genesis 46:2, NIV). And He talked to Joshua and Samuel and David and Solomon and Daniel and Paul and all the others who lived confidently in the Lord.

And we think that if God spoke audibly to us, we too would live confidently in the Lord. We'd catch the spirit of Abraham and Moses and Daniel and Peter and John and Paul. We'd proclaim His name and spread His love. *We'd believe!*

But then something in the back of our minds (or is it our hearts?) begins to stir. And the discussion begins.

"What would you like?"

"I'd like to hear God's voice."

"Why?"

"So my faith will be strengthened."

"Do you remember what faith is?"

"It's believing."

"Believing in what?"

"Things not seen."

"Is that all?"

"And not heard."

"Yes."

"But He was *always* speaking to Moses and Samuel and Daniel and—"

"And all *they* had was His oral Word. You have His written Word."

"Why does it have to be this way?"

"Do you remember the test this world is undergoing?"

"Yes."

"Do you remember the accusation?"

"The one about God not playing fair?"

"Yes. Do you *want* Him to play fair?"

"Yes. But it's so hard sometimes."

"He said He's going to prepare a place for you . . ."

"I really need Him sometimes."

"And if He's going to prepare a place for you . . ."

"I need Him *now*."

"He *will* come again."

"And then the phone will ring?"

"No, then the trumpet will ring."

"For this very reason, make every effort to add to your faith . . ."

WHEN YOUR BOAT ROCKS
Victor Czerkasij

"He got into the boat and his disciples followed him" (Matthew 8:23, NIV).

Our flight from Seattle to Atlanta passed smoothly. Only a single strong bump of turbulence interrupted the ride. It kicked in the "Fasten Seat Belt" signs and caused everyone to giggle nervously. My wife, Rene, and I felt glad to be near the end of another camp meeting assignment and on the way home.

I had been so worried that my son, Alex, would cry throughout the flight that I had suggested we buy something like Dimetapp, which causes heavy drowsiness. Rene protested: "We will not be drugging our baby!"

"Honey, I was thinking of buying it for myself," I answered gently.

After a short stop in Atlanta to change planes for Chattanooga, we lifted into the air for the last leg of our journey. It was 11:15 p.m.

Just three minutes into the flight, the pilot directed the flight attendants to buckle in and suspend any attempts at cabin service.

"Folks, radar shows a few storms between us and Chattanooga," he drawled, "but we'll be on the ground in 20 minutes." He hadn't put down the microphone for 10 seconds when the first flashes of lightning began to illuminate our windows. And this wasn't the occasional passing bolt of lightning that most of us see in storms. Instead, we appeared to be heading through the final minutes of a Fourth of July fireworks display combined with a bombing raid on Berlin.

"A furious squall came up, and the waves broke over the boat" (Mark 4:37, NIV).

The shaking began. Our MD-80's wings flapped up and down, and we gripped one another as the plane bucked like a rodeo bronco. Cowboys fly about 10 feet in the air, but we were thousands of feet up and twisting and turning in what we guessed were maneuvers to evade the storm.

About 40 minutes into our 20-minute flight, the pilot assured us that the worst was behind us. He apologized for the torment and explained that this storm had mushroomed into something bigger than any radar could have shown. "We can't go back to Atlanta, and Knoxville and Nashville are shut down, so Chattanooga is still our desti—" He was cut off by the alarms now plainly sounding from the flight deck as we dropped like a rock. This was classic wind shear.

Rene becomes talkative when she feels nervous. I grow silent as the grave. The two of us had last experienced this dichotomy during a category 5 hurricane, and, before that, on our wedding day.

This time Rene began to claim Scripture. Her mind remained as sharp and clear as ever, and the Bible verses poured forth in a stream. I had never been more comforted by those words. They were life. They were power. They were complete assurance. And I did not want her to stop for a moment's breath.

The pilot now had the plane in a nose-forward dive to gain speed and to rebuild a thrust of air under the wings.

"[but] Jesus was . . . sleeping" (verse 31, NIV).

Rene gripped my hand and squeezed. She smiled and said with absolute simplicity, "At least we'll go together." She uttered this even though she was expecting our second child and sitting next to me, her husband, while our firstborn slept oblivious in his father's arms.

"The disciples woke him and said to him, 'Teacher, don't you care if we drown?'"
(verse 38, NIV).

Was the pilot watching the altimeter? Could he see how low we had plummeted? Wasn't Lookout Mountain hulking out there somewhere?

Slowly the nose crept upward, and the engines revved ever higher. Fellow passengers, chalk-white and silent, mentally urged the turbines to greater power. Alex fidgeted in my lap and gave a fitful snort, still deeply asleep. And the voice of God continued to speak through His Word, which was embedded deeply in the mind of the woman sitting next to me: "Be strong and courageous. Do not be afraid or terrified . . . , for the Lord your God goes with you; he will never leave you nor forsake you" (Deuteronomy 31:6, NIV).

"He said . . . , 'Why are you so afraid? Do you still have no faith?'"
(Mark 4:40, NIV).

Why was I so afraid? Why had my usually glib tongue frozen to the roof of my mouth? Where were all *my* Bible verses? Could it be that in the time of calm I had made my God a side order while all the time He should have been the main course?

How often I had placed Him in the role of a fire extinguisher in the corner of my heart; relaxed to know of His presence but otherwise content to let Him gather dust. Now, in a 10-alarm blaze, I could not rely on another's study to pull me through. What should come through in this time of crisis was the power of the relationship we had developed in times of calm. Did I have the right to seek His blessings now if I had chosen not to before? *Oh, God, have mercy on me, a sinner . . .*

"He got up, [and] rebuked the wind and . . . the waves. . . . And it was completely calm" (Mark 4:39, NIV).

The jet circled the airport and lined up for another approach. We had been in the air for more than an hour, lurching like an old truck on a deeply rutted road. The landing gear mercifully came open, and we touched down on Lovell Field, drained of emotion.

We read later that during that storm of June 26, 1994, meteorologists in the Chattanooga area measured a record 800 lightning strikes on the ground in one hour, and they guessed that the flashes in the sky numbered as high as 6,000 in that same period. A number of tornadoes had also touched down, causing four deaths. The rain had brought widespread flooding.

I wanted to be the last passenger off the plane. I achieved this because of the time it took me to uncurl my fingers from the armrests. Also, I wished to shake the pilot's hand and ask a question that seemed not at all stupid to me: "Were we ever in any real trouble?"

The perennial cockiness of a pilot, usually worn as a badge of pride, lay prostrate somewhere on the floor of the cabin as he looked me in the eye and answered quietly, "That was about the worst I've ever seen."

I looked over at Rene. Her face was aglow.

"They were [amazed] and asked each other, 'Who is this? Even the winds and the waves obey him!'" (verse 41, NIV).

Alex awoke and smiled.

POTLUCKS
Alex Bryan

I've learned a lot about potlucks over the years.

I suppose I should be careful what I say, since I've never actually *contributed* to any potluck that I can remember. You could say that I've "come along for the ride." Since Mom always brought food, I figured I was covered.

If your church is small enough, on potluck days the aroma of hot entrées invades the sanctuary and serves as a closing bell for the preacher. It's hard to feed the soul when the body's radar detects food.

I've learned that it is important to be a kid or sit at a table with kids, because kids always go first. They get to choose among all the dishes. Sometimes they pick on all the dishes. And if they use the same spoon for enough entrées, you can sample any entrée from any one dish.

Luck is the essence of potluck. If you visit my church in North Carolina the odds of a tasty meal are very good—Southern cooking is no fluke. Nevertheless every church is not so fortunate.

I learned the hard way that church potlucks require potluck etiquette. It's *always* rude to criticize potluck food. The odds are good that the cook is sitting next to you. Not only must you refrain from criticism, but you should not praise any one food on your plate. The absence of compliments for the other foods will get you in hot water with at least one woman or man at the table. I haven't decided if it's rude to ask the sure-fire cooks what they made and which containers hold their creations. I've memorized my mom's dishes for quicker accessibility.

A final tip I've learned about church potlucks: never delay your encounter with the dessert table. Balance the paper cup, the bigger paper plate, the little dessert plate, and the plasticware if you must. The early bird gets the best chocolate cake.

I think potlucks represent Jesus' brand of Christian community. Everyone gives something. Everyone receives something. Not like the Christmas office party game, in which each person brings only one gift and each person leaves with one gift. In potlucks each individual gives to many, and each person receives from many.

Christians have more to say to the world through their actions as a community than through espousing Scripture, avoiding temptations, and financing programs. The community of faith represents, albeit imperfectly, the way God's society works in heaven.

Many examples of the caring Christian community come to mind:

- A poor student has no clothes. The dormitory dean rallies the men in a collective offering that supplies new clothing for the schoolmate in need.
- A Sabbath school class rallies to send a child to a Christian elementary school. The Christ she will learn about is already revealed through the love of her Christian community.
- The pastor needs a break. He just can't afford to get away. The elders sense his need and together send their pastor and his wife on a vacation to renew his spiritual and emotional energies. The servant of God experiences God through the love of the Christian community.
- An elderly person cannot tend to her yard. A youth group, with mowers and shovels and rakes, manicures her lawn. Jesus is at work this day.
- A church of another denomination burns down. Since Sunday services will not conflict with the Sabbath services, the church offers its facility free to the disaster-bitten church.

One biblical moment in particular shows the spirit of Christian community. The scene has the potential to be a potluck. Trouble is, no one brought any food. Jesus has been teaching a crowd all day long. The sermon draws to a close. Now it's time to eat.

At this late hour, surrounded by hungry people, Jesus rounds up His 12 disciples and tells them to rustle up some food. "See what entrées the people have brought along and bring them to Me. We're going to have a potluck."

They go around the crowd without success. Finally Peter's brother, Andrew, discovers some food. Five loaves and two fish. It's a little boy's lunch.

I wish I had a snapshot of that moment. Andrew, arms outstretched, asks the boy for his yet-to-be-assembled tuna sandwich. The boy looks up at this stranger, somewhat puzzled.

"Jesus asked us to gather all the food we could. He's organizing a last-minute potluck. Your bread and fish are all we can find."

THE RIDE OF YOUR LIFE

The boy's look of squinty-eyed perplexity turns to wide-eyed excitement. He realizes what's about to happen. The people don't know. The boy's mother doesn't know. The disciples haven't been clued in. Only the boy knows what Jesus will do.

Jesus glances over at the boy with a twinkle in His eye. The boy beams from ear to ear and hops up and down. He can't wait to see this!

In the next few seconds a culinary explosion takes place. The once-doomed potluck becomes a smash. Jesus hands bread to the disciples, but they don't immediately fill their starving stomachs. They pass it to one person in each circle of hungry believers. The trick is to keep sharing. They divide the fish and they divide the bread. Again and again and again.

How appropriate that just hours before, Jesus had preached about honoring the Son (see John 5:23). A young son demonstrated what giving honor to the Son is all about: a genuine willingness to give what he could give. And *kaboom*. A miracle erupted, the community of faith became just that, and the Son of God was honored.

I've learned a lot about potlucks over the years. I've also learned a lot *from* them. Especially from one a couple millenniums ago.

"To your faith goodness . . ."

THIS LITTLE CONDITIONAL LIGHT OF MINE
Andy Nash

"Then Jesus told them, 'This very night you will fall away on account of me. . . .'
"Peter replied, 'Even if all fall away on account of you, I never will.'
"'I tell you the truth,' Jesus answered, 'this very night, before the rooster crows, you will disown me three times.'
"But Peter declared, 'Even if I have to die with you, I will never disown you.'
"And all the other disciples said the same" (Matthew 26:31-35, *NIV*).

*Y*ou've seen him at nationally televised football games. Especially during field goals. "The kick is up . . ." and there he is, in the crowd, the guy with the white placard bearing one brief message in red: "John 3:16."

You've seen her at campaign rallies, right in front of the cameras. "If elected, I will not forget who sent me to Washington . . ." And there she is, in the crowd, the one in the white T-shirt that reads in screaming orange, "Wake up, America! Prophecy is being fulfilled right before our eyes!"

You've seen them at airports, street corners, and colleges. Our colleges! They have old truths. They have new truths. They have messages for our eyes and words for our ears. Unashamed of their message, they are fervent about sharing it. They talk a lot and listen little. But they are holding up their Christianity high. They call themselves street evangelists. Their mission is America. And they don't care what people think of them.

❋ ❋ ❋

In July 1992 I returned from a year in Thailand as a student missionary. For one year I had taught English and Bible to hundreds of Buddhists, most of them my age. I had told Bible stories to those who understood English and performed Bible charades for those who didn't. I had sung "Peace Like a River" and "Side by Side" with my colleagues up front at our vespers programs. I don't like singing up front. I had crawled around on the floor like a big bear as a dozen Thai children took turns mauling me. Beautiful, smiling, punishing Thai children. And now I was back home.

THE RIDE OF YOUR LIFE

It felt strange—almost foreign—to be sitting at McNamara Pontiac in Orlando, Florida. The lounge TV showed *Good Morning, America*—in English. Next to me, a woman and her little boy argued about something apparently important to both of them—what time Barney the dinosaur would start on TV that afternoon. *Who's Barney the dinosaur?* I wondered.

Across from me sat a cute girl about my age, reading a magazine. She looked like she might be Thai. I wondered whether she had been to Thailand too.

Normally I wouldn't have struck up a conversation with a stranger, even if she were a cute stranger. But because I was single and bored with waiting for new tires to be put on my car, and because this girl looked Thai, I decided to risk it. I thought we might have something in common.

"Excuse me," I said. "Are you by any chance Thai?"

"No, I'm not," she replied without raising her eyes.

I decided never to be friendly to anyone ever again. Then she looked up, smiled, and said, "But a lot of people have asked me that before. My name's Pauline."

The next few minutes blurred by—something about Pauline (she was Filipino) just moving to Orlando and taking a job at Disney's Pleasure Island; something about her being a San Diego Chargers cheerleader the year before; something about me living in the Orlando area for years and being happy to show her around sometime. (Now, go easy on me: I'd been out of the dating scene for a while.)

Just as I was about to tell Pauline that I too had been part of a football organization (the Detroit Lakes Lakers in junior high school), the McNamara Pontiac mechanic walked in and said that the "car for Nash" was ready.

"Are you sure it's ready?" I asked the mechanic.

He said yes and told me to follow him out front to the cashier. *So much for Pauline,* I figured.

Four or five evenings later the phone rang at my house.

"An-deeee," my sister yelled from upstairs. "It's some girl named Pauline." I didn't recognize the name. *Pauline,* I thought. *Who's Pauline? I don't know anyone named—*

Then I remembered. *The cheerleader. She's calling me?* I hadn't expected to talk to her again.

I closed the den door downstairs, found my most casual voice, and picked up the phone. Five minutes later I hung up, thrust my fist into the air in victory, and went to ask my dad if I could borrow a few bucks for my dinner date the next night.

I was excited. I hadn't been on a date in a long time. That Pauline wasn't an Adventist didn't bother me. The way I saw things, Pauline was just a girl who happened to have been a cheerleader and I was just a guy who happened to have played tackle football—in seventh grade. What religion we were didn't matter. Besides, I reasoned, I had just put in a whole year as a missionary in Thailand. I should be allowed to go through one evening without being "different." The last thing I wanted to do was scare the cheerleader away.

I met Pauline the next night at a lakeside restaurant called Shooter's. We sat down at a small table by the window, and my test began almost immediately.

"So," Pauline said. "What were you doing in Thailand?"

"Uh, I taught English," I said. *And Bible*, I thought to myself. *I taught English and Bible.*

"Oh, really?" she asked. "Do you want to be a teacher?"

"I don't know," I said.

"What college do you go to?" she asked.

"Oh, it's a small private school in Tennessee," I said. "It's called Southern."

These questions were a real drag. Already I had twice played down my religion. I decided to ask Pauline a few questions instead.

"So," I said, "do you like working at Pleasure Island?"

"Yeah," she laughed. "I like dancing, and I *love* getting paid to dance. Do you like to dance?"

Man, I hated that question. Do I like to dance? No way. Even if our church *encouraged* dancing, I wouldn't do it. I'd feel so stupid. OK, I admit it. I tried dancing once in junior high, and I did feel stupid. Do I like to dance?

"Now and then," I lied, terrified she would suggest that we hop on down to the nearest disco.

Fresh from a year as a student missionary, I found myself worried about coming across like the fanatics who hold up placards. I was hiding who I really am and what I believe—hiding it under a bushel (I had promised, through the Sabbath school songs I'd sung as a kid, that I wouldn't).

By the end of an evening in which I cared more about impressing a girl than about the One who had created that girl, I had had enough hypocrisy.

"Pauline," I said as we walked to her car. "There's something—or, rather, some things—I should tell you about myself. I didn't mention that

I was actually a missionary in Thailand. I was there to teach English, but I was also there to teach Bible. I go to an Adventist college in Tennessee, and my religion is pretty important to me. I don't know whether you've heard of Adventism."

"Oh, yeah, I have," she said. "I had a friend who's Adventist. He's pretty cool. I'm Catholic."

We talked about our churches to end the evening. (I decided to avoid beast identification.) Then she got into her car and drove away, and I never saw her again. We weren't what you would call a perfect match.

I learned several lessons from my date with the cheerleader: total honesty works best; girls are more impressed when guys stand up for what they believe; and never, ever, deny the Lord. I found it easy to talk openly about my God and my church in a Buddhist country in Asia. Sometimes I felt like Paul in a hostile foreign land. But when it came to holding up my beliefs here at home, I acted more like Peter in his hometown. And I didn't need a rooster to inform me that I was out of line. My conscience alarmed me enough.

Certainly the way I played down my beliefs was wrong, but I don't think it's unusual. It's not fashionable to talk about religion in this country. And Adventists aren't exempt.

In February 1995 the *Adventist Review* ran a cover story entitled "What Does the Public Think of Us?" It reported some of the findings of a large study commissioned by the North American Division to learn what North Americans know about our church. The study found that:

- only 53 percent of North Americans recognize the name Seventh-day Adventist (that figure is down from 70 percent in 1980, 65 percent in 1970);
- only 21 percent say that they know an Adventist personally;
- 12 percent have visited an Adventist church;
- when those who are aware of our church were asked to name the first thing that came to their minds when they heard the name *Seventh-day Adventist*, three of the top 10 responses were "Mormons/Latter-day Saints" (number 4), "cult/sect/David Koresh" (number 7), and "far-fetched religion/fanatics" (number 10). Certainly not the image we would hope for.

The *Review* article closed with a question: "What practical ideas would you suggest to us on how to increase our denomination's name recognition and improve its public image?"

A worthwhile question. Certainly, with hundreds of thousands of

Adventists in North America, we should have more than 53 percent name recognition. The question is, How do we get it? A new comprehensive ad campaign? More parade floats? Updated evangelistic series with fewer beast posters?

These things might help, but they're not enough. Even today the *best* way to increase our name recognition and improve our public image is still the same as it's always been: day-to-day, one-to-one, tear-in-our-voice sharing of our message with those who haven't heard it.

Why? Because people forget mass-mailed literature and catchy billboards and Christmas Eve specials. What they don't forget is the moment, in an age of "loonies" screaming their messages at passing cars, when a friend takes them aside and shares the Source of real happiness, Jesus Christ.

We can, of course, share Jesus in many forms—a blessing at a restaurant; an acknowledgment for an accomplishment; a quiet example; a *consistent* devotion to the standards we know are right; sharing the truth about the Second Coming or the Sabbath day; a direct disclosure of the gospel itself—but He must be shared somehow. There is no right time or right place to play down what we believe. There's no way to know which moments are crucial and which are not.

I don't think God expects us to perch at street corners and shout the gospel at cars. And I don't think we'll reach the ends of the earth with cardboard signs at football games. But I'm sure of this: Each real opportunity we have to share His love with His children is a precious opportunity. And each time we deny or ignore or water down our relationship with Him, He feels that stinging betrayal of a close friend all over again.

"Now Peter was sitting out in the courtyard, and a servant girl came to him. 'You also were with Jesus of Galilee,' she said.

"But he denied it before them all. 'I don't know what you're talking about,' he said.

"Then he went out to the gateway, where another girl saw him and said to the people there, 'This fellow was with Jesus of Nazareth.'

"He denied it again, with an oath: 'I don't know the man!'

"After a little while, those standing there went up to Peter and said, 'Surely you are one of them, for your accent gives you away.'

"Then he began to call down curses on himself and he swore to them, 'I don't know the man!'

"Immediately a rooster crowed. Then Peter remembered the word Jesus had spoken: 'Before the rooster crows, you will disown me three times.' And he went outside and wept bitterly" (Matthew 26:69-75, NIV).

"To your faith goodness . . ."

A Few of My Favorite Things

Alex Bryan

*R*aindrops on roses and whiskers on kittens . . ."
Here are a few of my favorite *Adventist* things:

- Charles Bradford sermons
- Morningstar Farms Grillers
- springtime at Southern Adventist University
- the music of Take 6
- *The Desire of Ages*, chapter 1
- Aunt Sue and Uncle Dan
- CompuServe Adventists
- Loma Linda infant heart transplants
- anything written by George Knight
- Sabbath school
- sundown on Friday night
- the risk-taking pioneers (of the 1840s *and* the 1990s)
- *Uncle Arthur's Bedtime Stories*®
- academy teachers
- *Liberty* magazine
- the children's story
- GC sessions
- the three angels
- the Wedgwood Trio
- ADRA
- and most of all . . . the Advent hope

"To your faith goodness . . ."

COME AND GET IT!
Victor Czerkasij

On September 11, 1992, a category 5 hurricane with the cute name of Iniki smashed through the island of Kauai, Hawaii, while I lived there. With gusts clocking in at 175 mph and top recorded speeds of 227 mph turning some atheists into deists, not a whole lot remained standing after Iniki blew out to sea.

No electricity or phone service, little running water—and you couldn't just drive to another county unless you owned a hovercraft. When the marines arrived with the first airlifted water trucks, I drank like a dying man. Never mind that the lukewarm water tasted of chlorine and plastic. I took home all I could carry.

We stood for hours to buy outdated batteries and overripe fruit. And when mail service began again, I was ecstatic to find, in a family care package, a melted chocolate bar. We ate it slowly—sucked the almonds until the chewing urge took over, and licked the aluminum wrapper clean.

Why do you suppose we acted this way? We were hungry and thirsty. Lacking our simplest needs, we responded in a predictable manner—like refugees.

Jesus portrays our quest for the eternal kingdom of God as a search for a compelling need. A man discovers the perfect pearl and sells all he has to purchase it. Another buys an uninteresting piece of land and doesn't seem to mind if the price is high. He sells all he has. His family, undoubtedly suffering from coronaries at first, is speechless with joy when he reveals the treasure.

Acts 2 records a sermon, preached by Peter at 9:00 a.m. one day, that "pierced" the people "to the heart" (verse 37, NASB) and had them scurrying to baptism. Thousands had gathered to hear about Christ and did not want to leave. If only I had that kind of trouble after my sermons.

The key to understanding these folks' behavior is tucked away in Matthew 5:6: "Blessed are those who hunger and thirst for righteousness, for they will be filled" (NIV).

THE RIDE OF YOUR LIFE

What condition exists for those who desire righteousness? Hunger and thirst. Why is it, then, that when I arrive to lead a Week of Spiritual Emphasis, a camp meeting, or a youth rally, ready to share a feast from God, the common response I receive looks like a trout landed on shore—mouths agape and eyes unblinking? No hunger or thirst at all. How can I share the knowledge of goodness when there are no takers?

Here are three reasons people aren't hungry:

1. **Snacking.** What you put away between meals affects your reaction to the main course. Be honest: What are you filling up on that takes the place of the most nutritious knowledge available? If you find family worship an annoyance or prayer a burden, or have ever thought, *Oh, brother, not another Week of Spiritual Emphasis,* I have to ask: What would it take for you to be hungry for spiritual food?

Seems wild horses can't keep some away from *Monday Night Football* or the new release at the cinema. But mention vespers, and there's a thousand excuses not to go.

2. **Lack of exercise.** Do you routinely put to use what you already know is right? Can God share new light with you if you are not living up to the light you already have? If you think you are not progressing in your relationship with God, you should go back to where the drift began. You might find that you chose to let the walk become a sitting affair because God touched a spot you wanted left alone. Ask Him for the courage you need to get past this point. Plead for the strength only the Spirit can give. It may hurt. It may take time and tears. But muscle torn is muscle built.

3. **Anorexia.** When anorexia sufferers look into the mirror, what do they see? Fat. But what is their real condition? Probably thin, sickly, and starved—in no way the picture of good health. Christians with spiritual anorexia can't be filled until they recognize their true condition: slow starvation.

But I'm a good person! I haven't been convicted of any crimes! No, but we were never meant to compare ourselves with society. When we compare ourselves with God, the knees begin to bend.

Now, I would be rude to leave you and send you off to Andy or Alex, two gentlemen who never met a dessert they didn't like. So I'll tell you how to *develop* a hunger and thirst for goodness.

1. **Watch others eat.** Have you noticed that pulling out a pizza or home-baked cookies brings around hungry people? If I remember the commercials right, they feature excited, salivating people singing the praises of crab legs being broken in slow motion. They hope that you too

will break forth in song and traipse down to the nearest fast-food eatery, touched by the stimulus of their example.

Watching the satisfaction of other fulfilled Christians will bring you to the table.

2. **Exercise.** One reason I pursued a college degree was that I worked a little construction—just enough to know I didn't want to swing a pickax all my life. What I specifically remember is consuming enormous amounts of food and Gatorade and never being satisfied, all because I was working so hard. More carbs, more liquid, more nourishment—that's all I wanted.

Likewise, when you walk with Jesus Christ all day every day, you'll want more prayer and study than you ever thought you could take in. You won't feel satisfied until you have His presence at every moment.

3. **Love.** At times I have returned from a long trip, relaxed in my "luxurious" coach-class seat, eaten airplane peanuts and pretzels like some bull elephant, and ruined my appetite. I walk in the door with a "Honey, I'm home," and behold, my olfactory senses identify a lasagna dinner that Rene has labored on all day. Both boys are eager for Dad to say grace so that we can all begin the feast.

Seeing my family waiting for my response to their offering of love creates a hunger in me. It's not so much a physical growling in the tummy as it is a humming in the heart. I'm going to sit down and eat out of gratefulness for what they have done for me, and I will be more satisfied by their presence than by the sautéed mushrooms between the ricotta cheese layers.

So it is with the presence of my Lord and Master and His efforts on my behalf. I am content to put away my own desires if they don't correspond with His. This way, through the Holy Spirit's prompting and guidance, I trigger a hunger for God's goodness in my life.

An elderly man once approached me and said firmly that if I didn't preach specifically against drugs, sex, and rock and roll, my time with a particular youth group would be wasted. "Otherwise, how will they ever know Jesus?" he asked.

Simple. If we knew Jesus, we wouldn't have to worry about drugs, sex, and rock and roll.

> *"Jesus said, . . . 'But I, when I am lifted up from the earth,*
> *will draw all men to myself'"* (John 12:30-32, NIV).

"To your faith goodness . . ."

A Twentieth-Century Psalm

Andy Nash

The Lord is my Master. I'm the happiest dog around.
He hands me a corner of His toast at breakfast time.
He takes me for a *leash-free* run to the lake each evening.
He scratches behind my ears.
He doesn't scold me when I bark at other dogs; He just laughs.

Even though I can't understand a word He says (aside from
    "good girl" and "the vet"),
I am always thrilled to hear His voice.
For then I don't have to sit alone on the porch any longer.
The way He scoops me up and pats my head—it makes me feel special.

He takes me for a jeep ride in the presence of the cat.
He lets me crane my head out the window.
My tail is perpetually wagging.

Surely warm baths and rawhides will continue to be
    a regular part of my life.
And the sweet sound of that front door creaking open will never get old.

A Word to the Wise

Andy Nash

'd seen his kind before, plenty of times before. You have, too. If not on a Wednesday or Friday evening, then a Saturday morning. They're either going from the parking lot to the church or from the church to the parking lot. They're old. *Ancient.* They have gray hair or white hair. Or no hair. They're hunched over in such a fashion that you have to twist your torso to compensate for theirs. Traffic waits as they cross the street. Shuffling rapidly. All alone. A cane clenched in one hand. A Bible in the other.

I'd seen his kind before. But I'd never given his kind a second thought. Until recently.

A few Wednesday evenings ago I dropped Cindy off at her residence hall at Andrews University and headed for home. It was freezing outside, and I was more than ready for a warm pizza, a soft sofa, and the second half of the Bulls and Celtics. After all, Michael Jordan was *back.* I gathered speed alongside Pioneer Memorial Church, but prayer meeting had just dismissed and I had to slow down. People rushed out of the church in twos and threes. But one eased down the ramp alone. I watched him. White hair, black hat, three-piece suit. At least 140 years old. He held his Bible tightly against his chest, much like a man would hold a baby tightly, much like Simeon would have held Jesus tightly. He worked his feet in front of my car and aimed for the parking lot. Then I lost sight of him.

I haven't seen this man since, but I've been thinking about him a lot. Old, arthritic, and alone, he looked completely content with that Bible in his hands. And I've been wondering how the relationship between him and God had grown so strong.

How many times had he read the Bible all the way through? Did he read it in the morning or at night? or both? What was his favorite book? What was his favorite text? Which Gospel did he enjoy most? Had his Bible always seemed this important to him, or was there a time when he felt indifferent toward it? How many times had he put it on the shelf (you know, the one where it gathers dust), only to retrieve it in a time of crisis? At what point in his life did he go from merely reading about a lost sheep to recognizing he *was* that lost sheep? How many times had he smiled while reading it? How many times had he cried?

There is, of course, much I don't know about this old man's life and how his Bible fit into it. I don't *really* even know whether he cherished his Bible as much as he appeared to. Maybe he was just showing off. ("Look at *me*, everyone; I'm carrying my Bible to prayer meeting.") But I don't think he was. I think showing off was the furthest thing from his mind. Instead, I think this old man carried his Bible the way he did because, after all these years, it was still a lamp unto his feet, still a light unto his path, still his letter from Heaven, still his link to Jesus.

And I've been thinking how much I want what he has.

But who doesn't? Surely all of us do. We want to be so enamored with the Bible that we feel lost without it. We want to be like one of these grandmas or grandpas we hear about who know their Bibles backward and forward. We want the Bible to be our mind's relish and our soul's desire.

For many of you, it already is. As for William Miller long ago, the Scriptures have become your delight. After all, you would much rather listen to the psalms of David than to your favorite radio station. You would much rather dissect the church in Philadelphia than the Philadelphia Eagles. You like nothing better than an intimate hour with your Bible. A trip to the mall? No thanks, you have plans to trace Paul's first missionary journey. A Saturday night video? Forget it—you thought you'd curl up by the fire with Leviticus. Well, maybe not Leviticus. The point is, the Bible is no longer just a book your parents made you bring to summer camp; it's a book that guides your life. If this description fits you, if you have reached a real relationship with your Bible, then praise God. May it only increase.

But if you haven't, if you're still striving for that relationship, here are a few things you might keep in mind:

1. *The Bible must be treated like an important appointment.*

We're busy. No surprises there. People have always been busy. Yet, our little 1990s lives seem to be busier—and more competitive—than ever. We vow to slow down and make time for the "important things" just as soon as we reach the top—except that we never reach the top. Cable TV, the information highway (yes, Adventists On-line included), and the 19 magazines we subscribe to lobby for our time and attention. Plus, we have to choose a long-distance service: AT&T has been a reliable friend, but MCI will put it in writing. By the time we decide which gadgets will best simplify our lives, we hardly have time to live. Families are put on hold; devotions are temporarily out of service. It's not that we want to spend less time with our Bibles. We just do.

Not until we regard reading the Bible as highly as we do studying for a big test or preparing for a big job interview will we have a real relationship with it. Making a regular appointment (no, it doesn't have to be early morning) with it, and keeping that appointment, is the first step.

2. *The Bible should be read as a textbook, not a tabloid.*

Make no mistake—the Bible can be a tough book to understand. In an age of fast-food newspapers and reader-friendly mail, we're not used to obscure symbols (fiery wheels? living creatures? time, times, and half a time?) and hidden meanings. And just when we find a version or a paraphrase to our liking, some scholar condemns it. We're tempted to give up the process altogether. Which is exactly what Satan would like us to do.

Certainly some books (Genesis, Psalms, James) read easier than others (Ezekiel, Zechariah, Revelation). But the secret to understanding difficult passages is the same as it's always been: hard work and prayer. Hard work means responding to the Bible in the same way we'd respond to a textbook—by writing in its margins or in a notebook, by using appropriate study guides (concordances, the Bible Amplifier series, and the Spirit of Prophecy), and by forming study groups to discuss what we understand and what we don't. Prayer means prayer.[1]

3. *The Bible wasn't written by John Grisham or Danielle Steel.*

Many of the things we read these days are written in a compelling style. The Bible, for the most part, isn't.[2] But that doesn't mean we should trade it in for a cheap novel, or even an expensive one. Nor does it mean we shelve the Bible and rely on the local Christian bookstore instead. Not that reading Lucado and Dobson, Swindoll and Campolo, isn't good; it is. These talented writers amplify Bible truths with modern-day anecdotes. So do many Adventist authors. Read these books. Enjoy them. But don't abandon the original. No book carries God's blessing as the Bible does. No book's even close.

And, though the Bible may not serve as a model of perfect writing, it does have its moments. Consider a few of the stylistic touches in the Gospel of John.

Parallelism. "He was in the world, and though the world was made through him, the world did not recognize him. He came to that which was his own, but his own did not receive him" (1:10, 11, NIV).

Humor. "So Peter and the other disciple [John] started for the tomb. Both were running, but the other disciple outran Peter and reached the tomb first" (20:3, 4, NIV).

Hyperbole. "Jesus did many other things as well. If every one of them were written down, I suppose that even the whole world would not have room for the books that would be written" (21:25, NIV).

Good stuff for sure. And if stylists like John (and David and Solomon) had written the whole Bible, it certainly would have been beautiful. But not complete. Thanks to journalists like Moses and Luke we get history to complement feelings. By using roughly 40 different writers to compose the Bible's 66 different books, God inspired a work with many styles and many perspectives so it could reach a people with many needs and many personalities—like us.

4. *The Bible is still relevant and still reliable.*

As the Bible itself predicted (see 2 Timothy 4:2-4) more and more people treat it as a story from the past, not a message for the present. This misconception might be blamed in part on our leaders. When a pastor (or an author) delivers a message with only a token reference to Scripture, what are we supposed to think?

"We need preaching today," writes General Conference president Robert Folkenberg, "that not merely encourages Adventists to study the Bible but that is biblical itself."[3] Not that every idea must be supported with 20 Scripture references, but it had better be founded in Scripture.

Even more serious than ignoring Scripture is doubting its authenticity altogether. In the past two years, both *Time*[4] and *Newsweek*[5] have run lengthy stories on the growing number of biblical scholars who dismiss much of the gospels as myth. Spearheading this trend is Depaul's John Dominic Crossan. Crossan's *Jesus: A Revolutionary Biography* suggests much of our traditional gospel—including Jesus' virgin birth, His miracles, and His resurrection—is pure fiction. Instead, says Crossan, Jesus was merely a poor peasant with some radical ideas. His crucified body was most likely eaten by wild dogs.

Joining in the gospel-trashing are the 77 New Testament scholars who belong to the Jesus Seminar, a group that, twice a year, votes on which lines of Christ are authentic and which are not by casting color-coded beads into a box. At last count, 82 percent of Jesus' words had been judged inauthentic.

Of course, these "new insights" would hardly be worth mentioning— except that people are listening. Christian people. Adventist people.

Adventist teachers. Sometimes we can get too smart for our own good.

5. *The Bible never stops saying what it has to say.*

One of my English professors defined a classic as a work "that never stops saying what it has to say." This is certainly true of the Bible—unless we stop listening.

The biggest mistake we can make is to decide we're done reading the Bible. No one's ever done reading the Bible. Not the theologian who has read it 40 times, not Billy Graham, not Mother Teresa, not Victor Czerkasij, not Alex Bryan, no one. The "magic" of the Bible is not in having read it, but in reading it regularly. For a couple reasons.

First, we're not camels. We can't just fuel up with the Bible one year of our lives (or one day of our week) and then coast—no more than we can douse ourselves with mosquito repellent in the spring in Minnesota and think we're set for the summer. (Believe me—it won't work.) A steady, *balanced* dose of the Bible is the dose God prescribes (see Matthew 4:4). He created our minds, and He knows what they need.

Second, each time we read the Bible, we read it a little differently. The text that didn't strike you yesterday may well strike you today. It may even change your life. Max Lucado tells of the time he discovered in Mark 7 that Jesus "sighed" at the sight of a deaf and mute man. For Lucado, that sigh meant comfort—comfort in knowing that, like us, Jesus also shakes His head and sighs at life's hurts. That sigh strengthened Lucado's relationship with Jesus.[6] The same can happen with you and with me. Our relationship with and understanding of Jesus will be strengthened as we read His biography. But when we don't, it won't.

Second only to prayer, what our church needs more of today is the same thing our church has always needed more of—careful, consistent study of God's Word. When we "do what it says" (James 1:22), who can estimate the blessings that will follow?

In the meantime, we might do well to watch the old-timers. (If you're already old, watch someone older.) Watch how they hold on to that which is eternal (the Bible) because the temporal (their spouse's hand, money, good health) has vanished. Watch them shuffle in and out of prayer meeting. Watch their calm faces. Watch their love for God's Word, and then follow their lead.

Some are getting an early start.

This past weekend I sat in on a kindergarten Sabbath school class. After we had sung songs and performed a skit and petted a visiting Akita, the teacher began to tell the story of Jesus washing His disciples' feet.

THE RIDE OF YOUR LIFE

"When Jesus came to Peter," said the teacher, "Peter didn't want Him to wash his feet. But then Jesus said that to have a place in the kingdom, Peter had to have his feet washed. And—"

"And then, and then—" chimed a 5-year-old boy with a big grin. "And then Peter said, 'Not just my feet, Jesus, but my head and my body, too.'"

We were astounded that this little guy had remembered such a small detail from the Bible. (His parents no doubt played a part.) And as he sat there, face beaming, I couldn't help but think, *There he is, "sitting among the teachers, listening to them and asking them questions."* [7]

I'd seen his kind before.

---

[1] See *The Great Controversy*, pp. 599, 600.

[2] Alex (Mr. Greek and Hebrew) reminds me that much of the Scriptures' stylistic beauty has been lost through translation.

[3] "Needed: Biblical Preaching." *Adventist Review*, Mar. 3, 1994, pp. 14, 15.

[4] "Jesus Christ: Plain and Simple." *Time*, Jan. 10, 1994, pp. 38, 39.

[5] "A Lesser Child of God." *Newsweek*, Apr. 4, 1994, pp. 53, 54.

[6] See *God Came Near*, pp. 63-66.

[7] Luke 2:46.

"And to goodness, knowledge . . ."

EGW

Alex Bryan

*B*ob Edwards, anchor of National Public Radio's *Morning Edition*, spoke to a collegiate audience a couple years ago. Following his remarks, Edwards fielded questions. One question captured my attention: "So, Mr. Edwards, what do you think of Rush Limbaugh?"

"I think he's a hoot," Edwards said. "But Rush Limbaugh is in a different business than I am. I'm in the news business. Rush is in the entertainment business. What Rush does is take a little bit of truth and stretch it . . . and stretch it . . . and stretch it." He lifted his arms and moved them farther and farther apart.

Rush Limbaugh often takes a "sound bite" and uses it in ways the voice behind the sound bite did not necessarily intend. But Rush is not alone. The news media, from CBS to *Newsweek*, have become expert at sound bites. A one-hour interview with CBS becomes a one-minute blip on the evening news. A two-hour speech becomes a short quote in tomorrow's *USA Today*. We live in a sound bite society. But do we really *understand* what was said?

In my twenty-fifth year as a Seventh-day Adventist and in my seventeenth year of Seventh-day Adventist education, the Adventist media (teachers, school administrators, preachers, parents, Sabbath school teachers, classmates) have quoted one person more than any other: Ellen G. White. I heard some quote as much as a page; others, no more than a word. But quoted she was, and quoted she is. With her writings available on CD-ROM, quoted she will continue to be.

If you're like me, your opinion of our church's prophet varied a lot growing up—from apathy to frustration to respect to excitement. Mine has depended on the most recent quote to reach me. She could be the mean old lady or the sweet grandmother. She could be the harshest judge or the kindest advocate.

So who is Ellen White? How does she fit into an Adventist Christian's spiritual journey? Will the real Ellen G. White *please* stand up!

THE RIDE OF YOUR LIFE

As a typical Baby Buster, I'd like the answer right now, thank you. I'd like a short, concrete explanation—perhaps in the form of an infomercial between MTV's hottest hits. In fact, following a brief *who*, give me a list of *whats*. You know, *what* she says about jewelry and *what* she says about the Sabbath, and *what* she says about the end of time.

Baby Busters, beware! A quick fix takes us into the minefield of sound bites. To hear a sermon in which Ellen White is quoted, to read a book that draws from her writings, to hear a church member use her to prove a point—these are limited experiences. Instead I offer an approach that has begun to work for me: *reading her for myself*. I don't mean playing with the CD-ROM or collecting quotations on a given subject. I don't even mean studying her writings with theological zeal. Reading her for myself means simply *reading*.

In college I studied history. Two professors taught the majority of my history courses. Both were exceptional: well-prepared, thorough, insightful, and challenging.

One day the history department received word that Arthur Schlesinger, Jr., advisor to President John F. Kennedy, would be speaking at the University of Tennessee at Knoxville. As history buffs living just a couple hours away, we history majors and our professors planned a trip to hear this significant American personality.

We sat up front and waited through seemingly endless introductions until the man himself, Arthur Schlesinger, Jr., began his lecture. For nearly an hour he talked about the Bay of Pigs, the Cuban missile crisis, domestic change in the early 1960s, and many other topics of the Kennedy administration. For nearly an hour we sat riveted to Schlesinger's every word.

Though our professors had given competent lectures, something made Schlesinger different. We had not just heard *about* the players in American history; we had heard *from* one of them. Listening to Arthur Schlesinger, Jr., was like watching a sporting event *live*. The smells of grass, peanuts, and 50,000 screaming fans is *live*. The feel of sunshine, cool breezes, and violently shaking stands is *live*. The thrill of hearing the crack of the bat, cheering crowds, and the p.a. announcer is *live*. There's just something special about being there. My living room Lazy Boy and 19-inch television just don't cut it.

This is what I've discovered about Ellen White. In secondary encounters with the prophet, you miss the "live" experience and the potential prophetic impact on your life.

One of the best things about being an Adventist is that God gave a prophet to *our* special niche in the Christian family. As a member of the newest generation of adult Adventists, I am thrilled Ellen White helped found this church. I am thrilled she wrote prolifically and prophetically. I am thrilled she wrote about Jesus Christ and me.

It would be easy for this generation of Adventists to discount Ellen White. It would be easy to discount her because her gift has been used as a curse. It would be easy to discount her because she wrote in another time and needs to be read in that historical light. "All I need is the Bible" would be a nice, easy approach. But, my fellow soon-to-be-twenty-first-century Seventh-day Adventist Christians: to discount her would be to give up an incredible gift.

Her gift includes a compelling case for the steady and never-changing God throughout history. From the beginning of *The Great Controversy* in heaven to its conclusion, God's hand stays on the wheel. If I've read it for myself I cannot help feeling His hand on the wheel in my life. Confidence in the past, present, and future is not something I'd like to give up. Ellen White helps me keep it.

Her gift includes a day-by-day walk with Jesus, *The Desire of Ages,* from His birth to the most important weekend in history. To sense a love from God so deep and true is something I'd rather not lose just because I've heard "but Ellen White says" once too often. To lose that kind of love isn't an option. Ellen White helps me experience God's love.

Her gift includes hopeful *Steps to Christ,* steps to the best relationship I will ever have, a relationship I'd like to have for eternity. The great thing about these steps is that you don't climb up to meet the Saviour. Instead you come down from the hopeless platform of this world into the arms of a God who did the climbing on Calvary. Ellen White reminds me that God is approachable.

Her gift includes stories of *Patriarchs and Prophets,* kings and apostles, and an incredible *Story of Redemption.* The prophet strengthens your spiritual journey.

Our generation can read Ellen White. Why let another person's misuse ruin an incredible experience? We can allow the prophet's contribution to enrich our lives and our church. The spiritual potency of Ellen White's prophecy must be a force in our future. The effectiveness of *our* movement will depend on it.

"And to goodness, knowledge . . ."

GOD AND MY GIRLFRIEND
Victor Czerkasij

One of the nice things about being older is telling others not to worry so much. One of the irritating things about being younger is *hearing* that you shouldn't worry so much. Right now I fall in a nice balance somewhere between the two. I'm not so far along in life that seeing a 16-year-old breaking up with his girlfriend doesn't remind me it can hurt. On the other hand, neither would I knot the rope for the guy to hang himself.

But my life wasn't always so neat.

When I was 18 and a freshman in college, my blond girlfriend of three years gave me the pink slip to our relationship. I'm talking major walking papers. *Fini*. The end.

That was a memorable day in the history of clichés. She said that I was *a great guy* and that *I would make some lucky girl happy one day*. She would *always remember me for being sweet*. And, of course, let's not forget the classic *we can still be friends*. Right.

The reason she gave for going her own way: I relied too much on her rather than being the leader. More specifically, she planned to marry someone who knew God from a personal relationship and could guide a household by drawing on that strength. Better that we part now, she thought, than to find ourselves in conflict later in marriage.

Not a leader? No strength? I responded as many men would in a similar predicament: Like the whipped puppy I was, I begged her to return. I promised that I would change if she was willing to give it one more chance. She wouldn't, and I was alone.

Well, not exactly. With more than 600 guys in the men's residence hall, it's difficult to be alone. Makes it tough to find a place to cry. I sat on a small hill that overlooks the campus and let the lights from the tennis courts and the lampposts blur through the tears. I squinted tightly to make new visual effects and forgot for a moment why I was up on the hill.

Naturally, as you sit there, you blame God. I say "naturally" because I had only a passing knowledge of Him at the time. (He's really smart. He's everywhere. He knows when you've been bad or good, so be good for goodness' sake.) First I blamed Him for not understanding me. If He knew what would make me happy, then He would not allow such bad things to happen. After all, if it makes you happy, it must be good.

Next, I reasoned that if He *did* know it made me happy, and *still allowed it to be taken away*, then that's not even nice. Actually, it's downright mean. After all, at that moment no one on the entire earth could have been suffering as I was. I might hear about Bangladesh being wiped out by a typhoon or an African country hit by famine and think that was sad, *but, hey, I bet they never had such a neat girl leave them!*

Then darker thoughts came up. Here I crept through an unfamiliar realm. I toyed with the idea that maybe He doesn't exist after all. I thought there was the slim hope that God hears the challenge and instantly appears to grant three wishes to gain your good favor.

By this point my clothes were damp from the evening dew. I was thinking that I really ought to be studying, when a Bible story flashed into my mind. Evening. Dew. Doubting God. Gideon. The fleece.

Perfect. If, in Judges 6, God had revealed His will in a manner that a human being chose, why shouldn't He do it again? Wasn't this what my academy Bible teacher meant when he said we should claim God's promises? (I never heard what he actually meant. Too busy passing notes.)

What should I ask for? Fire from the sky? No, the college administration would get upset. Earthquake? *Really* upset. Lift me up somewhere high? Scared of heights. I stared at the lights of the quiet stars.

"Now, Lord," I prayed, "I've really been hurting. I know that I haven't always been the most faithful in my prayer life, but this time I'm really serious. This is a great chance for both of us to find out about each other. If You would only show me how much You care by sending a big, flaming shooting star across the sky when I say 'Now!' I'll know how much You love me and that You truly do exist. Please get ready, Lord, because I'm about to say it."

I waited a moment. Licking my lips, I whispered, "Now."

Nothing.

Maybe I had not given Him enough time to prepare. He might have been busy with Bangladesh. So I waited a minute more and prayed, "This is Victor again. Czerkasij. I'm waiting here patiently, so here we go again. If You're *really* there, if You *really* love me, then show me with a shooting star *now!*"

Silence. Stillness. A breeze stirring in the trees; a cricket chirping, mocking me.

But something did happen.

A thought whispered in my mind: "If you really love Me, then why don't you find out more about Me? Why were you so busy passing notes?" Until then, I had been asking the questions. "Can you, Victor, remember a time when someone questioned Me with a series of If's? He knew who I was. He knew what I could do. He just didn't love Me. And he fell from heaven." This was serious. I really didn't want to be put in the same league as *that* fellow.

One more question came through. "Do you remember how I answered *him*?"

Sure, I answered. *You answered Satan through Scripture.*

Here God made His final point. "Then it's through Scripture that you will learn of My love, and My will, for you."

I had never thought of that.

Back in the room I blew the dust off the cover and began to read. I half imagined that the authors wrote directly to me.

"No discipline seems pleasant at the time [Victor], but painful. Later on, however, it produces a harvest of righteousness and peace for those who have been trained by it" (Hebrews 12:11, NIV). *It's not a pleasant time to be alone, but I guess I'm not by myself since I have You.*

" 'Even now,' declares the Lord, 'return to me with all your heart, with fasting and weeping and mourning. Rend your heart and not your garments. Return to the Lord your God [Victor], for he is gracious and compassionate, slow to anger and abounding in love, and he relents from sending calamity'" (Joel 2:12, 13, NIV). This is good stuff! I had never pictured God as being the lonely one. He wants *my* company, just as I wanted time with this girl. I had never thought of that, because I was so busy wanting to please her and myself.

"Philip [and Victor] said, 'Lord, show us the Father and that will be enough for us.' Jesus answered: 'Don't you know me, Philip [and Victor], even after I have been among you such a long time? Anyone who has seen me has seen the Father'" (John 14:8, 9, NIV). Ouch. That must have really hurt Jesus. Here He reveals the Father so eloquently and still one of His own denies Him. To put God to the test like that, to place God on the terms of a human being, is so, so . . . familiar.

He has long forgiven me for my sullen, rash remarks. I learned that God does care for me. He began to care before I was born. He has a plan, which He discloses instantly to some like Gideon, over time to others as He sees fit. I trust Him enough now to say that.

We've come a long way since, God and I, and, no denying it, we still have a long way to go. But all that matters is that we're together. I spend a part of every day with Him for the same reason I wanted to be with that girl: I couldn't think of anything that would make me happier.

Years later I woke up one morning about 5:00 and ate a cereal and banana breakfast. I read a portion of the Word, spoke with my heavenly Dad, and then headed out to my blue VW around 6:30. I saw an otherworldly dawn on our island of Kauai, where I was teaching Bible. To the far east the sun reached out its rays of light. In the far west the blackness of night stubbornly clung to the sky while pinpoints of stars flickered through. Dew rested on the grass. I smiled as I thought of that evening some 10 years before, when I doubted God's love and His plans for my life.

Say, Lord, I thought. *Just for fun, would You mind if I received that shooting star this morning? For old times' sake.*

You couldn't miss it—looking like a supernova at first, there in the darkness of the night sky. But soon it curved, roaring east into the sun. I could very nearly hear the crackling of the flaming orange tail flowing many miles behind it. I followed it for the few seconds of its life as it arched into the rising of the sun, which by now had peeked its forehead over the rim of the Pacific. *Thanks, Father,* I thought, with great calmness. *That was a good one.* I drove down the gravel road.

And the girl? I ended up marrying her. Yes, God chose to give me the desire of my heart. Of course, whether He gave me that or not didn't make a difference. I was already satisfied to have the Desire of Ages.

HAVE YOU EVER NOTICED?

A n d y   N a s h

*H*ave you ever noticed that being as conservative as possible with yourself and as liberal as possible with others works best?

Have you ever noticed that some Adventists still say "Amen!" when someone mentions the idea of state-sponsored prayer in public schools?

Have you ever noticed that you enjoy church and Sabbath school a lot more when you participate?

Have you ever noticed that those who witness by debate don't hold a candle to those who witness by example?

Have you ever noticed that when a pastor warns against smoking or excessive TV watching or listening to rock music, the loudest "Amens" come from those who don't struggle with those particular problems?

Have you ever noticed that those most apt to criticize are often those most unwilling to help?

Have you ever noticed that the minute we stop brainstorming, we fall behind?

Have you ever noticed how we tend to avoid some Bible passages—such as those about tongues, exorcism, and freedom from the law?

Have you ever noticed that Sabbath afternoon naps seemed so boring when you were a kid, but so inviting now?

Have you ever noticed how some Adventist pastors borrow extensively from non-Adventist authors—Lucado, Campolo, Dobson—without giving them proper credit?

Have you ever noticed that the best way to keep from lying is not to do anything you'd have to lie about?

Have you ever noticed how we downplay the status of our national leaders until they are photographed with one of our church leaders, at which point we publish that photo in our magazines?

Have you ever noticed that other churches talk about being persecuted in hell and that we talk about being persecuted on earth?

Have you ever noticed that being Adventist *some* of the time will win people to the church *none* of the time?

Have you ever noticed how something relatively small—which worship format is right, how to improve our image, the meaning of the "daily," wedding bands—can seem so big until someone we love dies?

Have you ever noticed how easy it is to forget that Someone who loves us died?

"And to goodness, knowledge . . ."

THE WISDOM OF JESUS
Alex Bryan

"Jesus increased in wisdom" (Luke 2:52).

*H*ow?
I wonder if Jesus whipped the older folks at Trivial Pursuit. I wonder if He could predict the weather. I wonder if He could figure out crossword puzzles really fast. I wonder if He got A's from His mother-teacher, won the Nazareth spelling contest with Z-e-r-u-b-b-a-b-e-l, and could spot good wood from bad wood that suppliers tried to sell His father, Joseph.

How exactly was Jesus *wise?*

I witnessed the Supreme Court in session a few summers back. After waiting in line for two hours, passing through metal detectors, and reading my copy of the "Behavior Code" provided by a security officer, I took my seat in the hallowed chamber. Promptly at 10:00 a.m. a tone sounded and everyone stood. Nine black-robed judges appeared from behind a majestic curtain and sat behind the bench.

Wow! This is serious business! I thought.

One judge after another read decisions they had made on various cases. Each cited constitutional, historical, or legal precedents. The rationale presented in each case was obviously carefully considered. I watched the other judges listen. They seemed deep in thought— either about what their colleague was saying or some other weighty matter. They knew the law, and they knew how to apply it. They were incredibly wise.

The only story from Jesus' childhood is recorded in Luke 2. Jesus, at 12 years of age, goes to the Temple with His family for Passover. After the festival Mary and Joseph head back without Jesus, thinking He's nearby. He's actually in the Temple, wowing the wisest men of Israel. The discussion must be good, because the party's over and the conversation lingers. Something about this young boy captures the attention of the Jewish supremes.

He knew the law. He knew how to apply it. He was incredibly wise.

Our church needs a generation of wise men and women. (Not just able to fill in the blanks of the Sabbath school lesson or identify the first and second beasts of Revelation 13, either.) Our church needs us to *know* the law and how to *apply* it as Jesus did.

The Pharisees had memorized the Torah. But Jesus allowed Scripture to fill His mind and soul in a different way. The Bible became the heartbeat of His existence. It became the guide to discern His Father's will for *His* life. The Bible's words were the intellectual and spiritual food that fueled Jesus' devotion to His Father. Wise Jesus was a committed convert to the Book. Period.

"And Jesus increased in wisdom." Have I? Have you?

ALWAYS HUNGRY, ALWAYS FULL
Victor Czerkasij

Among the classic moments in my life, I seem to have a number of entries under *humiliation*, particularly the *supreme* variety.

I brought my girlfriend from academy to my house one home leave. I was careful to stipulate to my parents, however, that she was just my "friend." By some amazing coincidence, she was also a girl. (My parents are of the old school, which teaches that one should not notice the opposite sex until one's late 20s.) They weren't fooled by my semantics, and played the role of gracious hosts to the hilt, which reflected the genuine kind of people they are.

To get better acquainted, we decided to head for the local pizza place. That meant kid brother and younger sister fighting over the front seat. Groaning inside but knowing that I wasn't allowed to drive and did not have the means to pay for the meal anyway, I accepted Dad's "Got-you-over-a-barrel-don't-I?" smile, which he had perfected during my 16 years on earth.

We enjoyed a pleasant meal. Mom, true to her promise, did not share stories of me as a kid, and Dad did not protest the extra toppings. Even my siblings had quit singing the song that had the girl and I sitting in the tree, *k-i-s-s-i-n-g*. In the end, it seemed too perfect an evening, and tragedy had to strike.

The people sitting at a table next to us stood up and left. Two slices of pizza they had not eaten remained sitting on a plate. The waitress came over and began clearing the table. My mother got her attention.

"Excuse me, dear," she said. "What will happen to that pizza?"

The waitress shrugged. "I'm going to throw it away." Mom smiled sweetly and reached out for the two triangles. "Then I'll just take that for you." With a flourish she wrapped them in napkins and dropped them in her purse. My head began to swim, and I slipped under the table.

My parents, survivors of the horrors of World War II, wonder to this day what in the world was wrong with my attitude. Their typical line to me in such situations was "When we were hungry, young man, we would be thankful if we had a bite of bread or a piece of potato in our soup."

I'd protest that I would be thankful too, but that the war had ended a half century before and they didn't have to keep living as if it were still going on. *Why take cold pizza from someone else when you could have hot pizza of your own right now?* was my thought. But they couldn't understand me any more than I could figure them out. That is, until I met Ben-Hadad, king of Aram.

Ben-hadad had the notion to take his army and march over to the city of Samaria. Back in his time it did not take a frontal assault to cause terrible harm. You just had to surround the city with your army and let nothing in and nothing out—an ancient forerunner of our trade embargo. The trick was to starve the people until they couldn't resist.

Second Kings 6 says that the famine in the city was "great," which, even for us, with no Hebrew language training, might translate as "highly disastrous." So serious was this siege that a donkey's head sold for 80 shekels of silver, or around $175. If you didn't have that much money, the merchants at the market were willing to sell you a half pint of dove's dung for five shekels.

I don't have to make it more clear—the people in Samaria faced starvation. When people starve, they will eat *anything*. They spend money on stuff no one would *ever* buy if it weren't for the famine. Even more amazing, the people must have reached a point during the siege when they considered this satisfying fare. "C'mon over, Phil! Look what Marge was lucky enough to buy!"

Jennifer Toth, a reporter for the Los Angeles *Times*, wrote a book called *The Mole People*. It's an eye-popping account of her travels under the mean streets of New York City. In the dank subway tunnels and abandoned underground shafts, she found whole societies of vagrants, lost youth, the helpless and angry, living in the most squalid conditions. For most of them it is a self-imposed exile, a prison of their own creation. And yet, to hear them talk, they are more free, more at liberty, than any of the street dwellers above them. "No one tells us when to wake up," they reason, "or when to go to bed." "We don't pay taxes and don't have to work. This is the life!"

Because of the smell generated by so many people living with little or no sanitary facilities and the sight of what their daily fare consists of, Toth was overcome by nausea at times. Her only relief came from climbing up into the relatively clean air of the Manhattan sidewalks. There, she reflected on the humanity trapped below. How could they be satisfied with a life they were never meant to live? Couldn't they see that the way they live is beneath them? Why couldn't they climb a little higher?

As, mentally, I berate the foolish mole people for scurrying about in the dark and snatching at scraps, I feel a cosmic tap on the shoulder. Someone greater, from the highest of all perspectives, reminds me of His intent for me. There's a yawning chasm between *who I am* and *what I was meant to be*. When I behold the Creator, I realize that for all my head-shaking at the pitiful shuffling in the tunnels, I too am a mole person.

Satisfied that as a Seventh-day Adventist my spiritual pedigree is intact (my cuisine Bible-based and my dress clean of any sin), I become accustomed to a religious life devoid of relationship. The one I serve is myself.

And the angels must weep. "He doesn't see *Him!* Why can't he climb a little higher?"

A young girl received that instruction some 150 years ago. "Ellen, look a little higher." As long as the people on the straight and narrow path fixed their eyes on Jesus, she was shown, there was little danger that they would fall off the path leading to the Master, except by their own choice. Only when they averted their eyes, when they searched for some scrap of self or a morsel from earth, did their feet leave the slender way.

I've heard that every heart has an empty space shaped in the letters G-O-D. What do you try to fit in your empty space? F-A-M-E won't fit. Neither will S-E-X, M-O-N-E-Y, or L-E-X-U-S, which has been a sore point with me, since my only car has 140,000 miles and no air.

In the end, I could have temporarily filled a spot here or there, but mostly I would have mangled the letters and hurt my heart. That empty space holds only what was meant to be there from the beginning: our Father in heaven. Not donkey heads or cold pizza, but the love of a Saviour.

DELAY OF GAME
Andy Nash

I think every college student does it at one time or another. And if some don't do it, others do more than their fair share. Believe me, I speak from experience.

Slacking. The term has different meanings for different people. For me, slacking tends to mean "putting off until the last possible moment, sometimes later, an activity that should have been done, or at least begun, two to three months ago."

I admit it. I was a slacker many times through my college years. A history test in three weeks? I began studying after two weeks and six days. A term paper due at the end of the semester—a good idea to begin now? Yeah, right. A Sunday afternoon study session? How about a Sunday afternoon tennis session instead?

I knew I wasn't the only student with a procrastination problem, because once in a while the school would offer a time management workshop, which, the posters said, would help students "avoid last-minute cramming," among other things. The workshop looked like a worthwhile idea, but I decided to wait and go to the next one.

Now, don't get me wrong. I wasn't lazy through my college years. I worked hard at my jobs and with the school paper. And my grades held up fine—A's and B's. (I include this paragraph because my mom and dad don't deserve to be known as the parents of a complete inadequate. *"Oh, hi, Mr. and Mrs. Nash. Ted and I read about your son. We're very sorry."*) But, try as I might, I just couldn't seem to get my schoolwork and studying done until the last possible day. Or night.

Near the end of my senior year I returned to the dorm from spring break, lugged my travel bags into the lobby, spun my little mailbox knob, pulled out my midterm grade report, and was welcomed back by an F in linguistics. Shock set in. An F? I had never gotten an F in my whole life. But now, with just a few weeks to go, I had an F in a class in which I needed at least a C to graduate. At a time like this, I knew just one thing to do—go find my friend and fellow slacker Rick and see what *he* had gotten in linguistics.

"An F," Rick said.

"Denny's?" I said.

"Denny's," said Rick.

Two nights later (the night before the biggest linguistics test of the semester), Rick and I phoned our respective girlfriends, Robin and Cindy, wished them sweet dreams, drove to the local Denny's, ordered some waffles, tore the plastic off our linguistics textbooks, and spent the next six hours (11:00 p.m. to 5:00 a.m.) studying. You might say Rick and I hit a low point in our college experience. Every so often we would glance up from our notes, look at each other, and shake our heads in disbelief. *Never, ever again.* Even we knew better than this.

Later that morning Rick and I sprinted to Brock Hall, took our linguistics test, stumbled back to the dorm, and died. Remarkably, we both did well on the test and finished linguistics with a C+.

No damage done, right? Not quite right.

Though I learned a lot of what I'd missed in linguistics by staying up all night at Denny's with a friend who had a similar midterm grade (and whose reaction, like mine, to a 6 out of 10 on a daily quiz was no longer disappointment but a hearty "All right!"), I could never get back many aspects of that class. I had waited nine weeks to involve myself, to participate in the discussion, to ask questions, to contribute ideas. And those nine weeks were gone forever.

The cost of waiting.

Now, maybe you haven't put off your schoolwork until the last minute. But I bet you've put off other things.

At the beginning of your junior year in high school you develop a grudge toward another student because he's a jerk in an intramural flag football game. All year the two of you don't talk or even smile at each other. You basically hate this jerk. Except that when the yearbooks come out, the jerk asks you to sign his book! Before you know it, you're writing halfway decent things to the jerk and even apologizing, and when he does the same and you become friends the last week of school, you both wish you had patched things up in September.

You're in love with someone, but just before Christmas she says something hurtful, and you figure, Why should I buy *you* a nice present? So you break up. Months later you can't stand being apart any longer, so you reach for the phone, dial the number, and say, "Hello, Kim? I miss you."

Turns out, she has missed you, too.

You're in up to your ears with a new job, and you haven't had the chance to call your parents for several months or visit them for several years. You know that they want to see their baby grandchild. As you and your spouse sit at the kitchen table and make plans to fly to Fargo, where they live, to visit this summer when things slow down at the office, the phone rings. It's your mom, and she's sobbing.

Like a delay of game penalty in football, we pay when we wait to study, to communicate, and to love. What about in our church lives? Is there a cost of waiting to become a true, committed Adventist?

Yes, I think so. I think people who don't grow up Adventist (and people who do grow up Adventist but only halfheartedly) really miss out. This is my perspective now as a 25-year-old Adventist, but I didn't always think this way.

Did you ever envy the thief on the cross? I did. Sometimes as an Adventist kid I thought that the thief on the cross pretty much had it made. Here's how I saw it:

Did the thief accept Jesus? Yes.

Will he be in heaven? Yes.

Did he do whatever he wished his whole life? Yes.

Do I get to? No.

After all, when the Vikings played on Sabbath, I didn't get to watch them. When my snowmobiling buddies began drinking, they stopped inviting me on their trips. And when holding hands on an academy campus just seemed like the thing to do, mean Adventist teachers wouldn't let us. And I was missing out.

Or so I thought.

Only later did I realize the benefits of growing up in the Adventist lifestyle. I'm glad I spent my childhood Sabbaths with my family rather than with a television. I'm glad my friends left me out when my standards didn't fit in. And I'm glad academy social rules that seem so rigid keep young hearts from becoming scarred.

As we get older, of course, we face new situations and new temptations. But the principle stays the same: Our church sets guidelines for the same reason our government makes laws—to keep its people out of trouble and at peace. When we defer implementing what we know into what we do, we put off grabbing real contentment. You know it, and I know it.

It's like the old theme song on the Carousel of Progress at Disney World. The mechanical family tells how great their lives are with such new technology as dishwashers, radios, and microwave ovens, the familiar music builds, and everyone, even the mechanical dog, sings that now is the best time of your life. (Hit it, Sport!)

Not a bad lesson. Just as the Carousel of Progress family uses the latest technology to make their lives easier, we will use our technology—our commandments, our doctrines, our beliefs—to make our lives happier. And we must use it "right here and now." If we don't, we're no better off than anyone else. What is truth worth if we ignore it? And what is a remnant people for if we don't stand out?

"When you make a vow to God, do not delay in fulfilling it. He has no pleasure in fools; fulfill your vow" (Ecclesiastes 5:4).

"Lord, remember me in Your kingdom." A last-minute, deathbed, thief-on-the-cross decision for the Lord can be a beautiful experience. But it should not be our experience. To wait any longer than this moment is to wait too long. And it's selfish.

Too many sinners—the non-Christian in college, the atheist in the workplace, the new-ager in his or her own mind—are hanging on their own crosses and looking from left to right for a better way. The least we can do is point them toward Another who hung on a cross long ago. But we can't point toward anyone when we just sit around, twiddling our thumbs.

And we can't make up for what we're missing now by taking a final exam later on. Life doesn't work that way. We're mistaken if we think it does.

"And to knowledge, self-control . . ."

A GREEN TRUCK AND A RED ACCORD

Alex Bryan

*I*n academy I worked for the maintenance department of a nursing home. I mowed grass, repaired geriatric equipment, changed light bulbs, painted walls, and supplied firewood for the stone fireplace in the dining room.

One day I took out the old green truck with the bold white words "PISGAH MANOR NURSING HOME" on the door to replenish the woodpile. My destination: a sawmill a few miles away. As I listened to eighties tunes on the radio and daydreamed about high school romance and North Carolina Tar Heel basketball, I noticed I had missed a turn. Slowing down, I steered into a circular driveway, rapidly looped around past the front of the house, and stopped at the conclusion of my U-turn. Seeing no traffic, I pressed my foot on the accelerator. The balding tires spun gravel until they got enough traction to put me back onto the road.

Two hours later I began to stack the wood into neat rows outside the nursing home. The routine of walking from the truck bed to the woodpile and back set me daydreaming again. Not until the intercom blared my name did I regain full consciousness.

"Alex Bryan, call extension blah blah blah." It was the administrator's number.

"Hello, this is Alex."

"Could you come down to my office, Alex?" Mr. Kidder was my supervisor.

"Sure, I'll be right down."

My heart beat a little faster as I made my way to his office. I knocked on the door and heard, "Come in."

"We just received a telephone call," the administrator said. "Were you driving the truck this morning?"

"Yes."

"A man is irate because the Pisgah Manor Nursing Home truck went flying through his driveway. He said whoever was driving the truck spun the tires, which threw gravel all over his driveway and front yard. He said the driver was reckless. What's the story?"

Gulp.

"I . . . I missed a turn. I didn't think I was 'flying' through his driveway. The tires are bald on the truck. It's easy to spin out. I think he's exaggerating." A long pause filled the room.

"OK, Alex. That's all."

I left the office to finish my wood stacking. *It's over*, I thought. *At best I'll be pulling weeds for the next two years. For sure my truck-driving days are over. Back to pushing the Lawn-Boy. I hope. It could be worse. I could be out of a job altogether . . .*

"As Jesus went on from there, two blind men followed him, crying loudly, 'Have mercy on us, Son of David!' When he entered the house, the blind men came to him; and Jesus said to them, 'Do you believe that I am able to do this?' They said to him, 'Yes, Lord.' Then he touched their eyes and said, 'According to your faith let it be done to you.' And their eyes were opened. Then Jesus sternly ordered them, 'See that no one knows of this.' But they went away and spread the news about him throughout the district" (Matthew 9:27-31, NRSV).

Another miracle from Jesus. No big deal. The supernatural seems so natural with Jesus that it seems natural to me when I read the Gospels: multiple healings, a few bread multiplications, a couple water flotation phenomena, and ("oh, by the way") the dead-raised-to-life episodes. Nothing unusual for the Bible-reading Christian who's seen these stories over and over.

On the surface it seems like just another miracle. But two miracles happen here, not one. Miracle number 1 is obvious: Jesus gives sight to blind men. Who wouldn't do that if they could? Miracle 1 is my kind of miracle. Did you catch miracle number 2? It's what the two blind men asked for: *"Son of David, have mercy on us!"* The miracle they request is mercy.

Mercy doesn't seem like much of a miracle until we remember the assumptions of the New Testament Jewish community. Their society presumed that the men received blindness because they deserved it. Hardship, whether physical, social, or financial, was a sure sign of sin. Poverty meant sin; leprosy meant sin; a wheelchair meant sin; blindness meant sin. And the greater the plague, the greater the transgression. It was never easier to distinguish the sheep from the goats.

Miracle number 2 scares me because church life hasn't changed much since the Pharisees ran the show. The church still tends to value justice over mercy. The miracle of mercy in a merciless world is no easy task.

I don't worry about what is impossible for me. But the second miracle scares me because I *can* perform this one. It's easy to say I want to be like Jesus when He turns tap water into premium grape juice. It's easy to say I want to be like Jesus when Peter's feet turn into jet skis or when an over-loaded net nearly sinks a fishing boat. It's hard to say I want to be like Jesus (and mean it) when the hard miracle—the one I *can* perform—confronts me: *"Have mercy on us, Alex Bryan!"*

Have mercy on us? Who needs mercy? Who doesn't?

- Arthur Ashe died of AIDS. He contracted the disease from a blood transfusion in heart surgery. Arthur Ashe was one of the classiest athletes of our lifetime. He fought for the underprivileged. He committed himself to the accomplishment of racial equality in South Africa. He lived as a devoted family man—father and husband.
- Magic Johnson is HIV positive. One day he will probably die from AIDS. He contracted the disease from multiple sexual encounters with so many women he can't count them. His fame, his good looks, his money, all were tools that brought women into his bedroom. Magic Johnson's immoral lifestyle caused his condition.
- In Miami, Florida, a 39-year-old woman is on vacation with her two young children and her mother. Driving on I-95, she accidentally gets off at a wrong exit and ends up after dark in an inner-city neighborhood. Another car bumps her from behind. She stops. She gets out of the car to inspect the damage. Two men in the car behind grab her purse, beat her, and *run over her* as her children and mother look on helplessly.
- Three major league baseball players are enjoying the days of spring training—playing ball in the daytime and relaxing and partying at night. The baseball players go out for some night fishing on a nearby lake. They don't come back. Investigators say their boat hit a wooden dock at perhaps 65 miles per hour, killing two of them and critically wounding the third. Alcohol was in the boat. They were drunk. The player behind the wheel was above the blood-alcohol level determined as legally intoxicated in the state of Florida.
- Children are consumed in the fires of Waco, Texas. They are victims in a catastrophe.
- David Koresh is consumed in the fires of Waco, Texas. He is the creator of a catastrophe.

It is no miracle for me to have mercy on Arthur Ashe, a 39-year-old crime victim and her family, and the children of Waco. They didn't deserve their plight. They didn't do anything wrong. It is a miracle of magnitude for me to have mercy on Magic Johnson, three drunken ball players, and David Koresh.

But even these are the easy ones. These examples are just the headlines. I will never personally interact with the faces that appear on CNN. The real tests are much closer. The mercy *challenges* are right at home. The church is full of sinners. The church is full of people who sometimes hurt the church, its members, themselves, or the lost who need to come into the church.

Where does mercy fit in?

- A church board spat breeds division: Those in favor vs. those against.
- Financial woes create a climate of finger-pointing.
- Generational warfare alienates young from old.
- Economic warfare alienates rich from poor.
- Gossip rips congregations.
- Self-righteous members prevent sinners who know their need from entering sanctuaries of sinners who don't.
- Worship style preferences become salvation (and damnation) issues.
- The local church jobs hierarchy promotes religious ladder climbing. The rungs become a battleground.
- Deacon A doesn't like what Elder B is doing.
- Member Y doesn't even like Pastor Z.

I have a thousand reasons never to be merciful. Let me heal the sick or something. But please, Jesus, don't make me be merciful. Mercy is hard. Mercy is the last thing I care to contribute to my church's experience. Let somebody else.

Jesus says: "Blessed are the merciful, for they will be shown mercy" (Matthew 5:7, NIV). But not only did He command it from us, Jesus lived it. He lived a life dominated by mercy—the essence of what it means to be a part of God's kingdom. From showing unusual compassion to a couple blind men to demonstrating irrational forgiveness on the cross, Jesus is all about mercy. His mercy overcame sin. His mercy for me is the only reason I'm spending eternity in paradise.

Guess what? Mercy for others is the only way the church will become paradise on earth. Sinfulness isn't going anywhere for a little while. Mercy must not either. The miracle of mercy, Christ's legacy to His church, is the miracle we must continually perform in the community of faith and the world. It's tough. The mercy miracle makes me think harder about wanting to be like Christ than any biblical standard. Mercy is the least likely response to sin. But mercy must be our response. Mercy will revolutionize our churches and make life outside the church substantially different from life inside the church.

Jesus wants us to plug mercy into our psyches. In the halls, boardrooms, classrooms, and sanctuaries of our churches Jesus wants mercy, rather than faultfinding, to be our "gut" reaction. Faultfinding is useless because fault is everywhere—in the world *and* the church. Grace-driven mercy is powerful because it deals with widespread fault in an intelligent, mature, and godly way.

At the nursing home I continued to move wood from truck to pile. That sick feeling of having done something wrong and getting caught stuck in my stomach. The cold winter air added misery to the feeling of aloneness inside me.

Once again the calling of my name over the intercom interrupted my thoughts. The administrator's voice. He wanted me to go to his office again.

My brief journey was nothing short of my own little trail of tears. Of course, the tears stayed inside—no male teenager cries in public. I knocked on his door.

"Come in."

"Mr. Kidder."

"Alex." I knew this was it.

"Alex, there's a nail in a tire on my new Honda Accord."

What? Am I responsible for this, too?

"I need a new tire."

Excuse me?

"Here's the key to my Accord. It's the new red four-door in the back parking lot."

I know; I've seen it.

"I'd like you to drive it downtown and get a new tire for me."

"You—you want me?"

"Yes, Alex."

Mercy, sweet mercy.

"And to knowledge, self-control . . ."

The Stockholm Syndrome
Victor Czerkasij

One of my wife's distant relatives is a police officer in a Western state. When we visited him one summer, I accepted his offer to let me ride shotgun on his 10:00 p.m.-6:00 a.m. shift. He promised me a bookload of adventures, and he delivered.

We chased a car thief, responded to a 7-Eleven holdup, and emptied a swimming pool of under-the-influence teenagers who had crashed the wrong home by mistake.

But the saddest experience was arriving at the home of a woman who had changed her mind about calling for us. She said she had had a misunderstanding with her husband and would we please leave? She spoke to us from the curb. Behind her, in the distance, sat the big lug, in shorts and tank top.

About an hour later we received a call from the same address. How the scene had changed: The wife's face was bruised and puffy, mostly blue and a little black. Blood ran under her eyes, and some trickled from her mouth. She stood on the front lawn crying while her husband cursed from inside the house.

More police officers arrived and wrestled the husband/batterer outside. As they grabbed his elbows and joined his wrists behind his back for the handcuffs, the wife, in one fluid motion, leaped up and smacked my distant relative on the face, shrieking, "Leave my man alone!"

In the seventies, in Stockholm, Sweden, terrorists took some hostages at a bank. During the crisis a strange relationship developed between terrorists and hostages: The hostages began to empathize with the terrorists! At one point some hostages offered to take up positions to protect the ones most likely to hurt them.

Perversely, the hostages had forgotten that the police were trying to rescue them and were not, in fact, the enemy. These poor people should have feared most the ones who had bound them with ropes and tied grenades to their waists. ("Yoo-hoo! Mr. Terrorist! I think my grenade is slipping. Could you tighten it?")

We all fall victim to spiritual Stockholm syndrome. When suffering befalls us or we reap the consequences of our sin, we try to shift the blame to God rather than plead with Him for the strength to bear the burden. Sometimes we excuse ourselves by blaming our genes, and sometimes we whitewash the effects of sin and downplay them.

Wouldn't it have been wonderful for Israel to admit to God, and to the prophets He sent to them, "You're right. Child sacrifices are, quite frankly, a terrible sin and should have no place in our lives. Forgive us, O God!"

Wouldn't it have been easier for all of us if Adam and Eve had said, "No, no, we both ate the fruit and we're guilty. There's no sense in blaming each other or You, O God."

What if some of the priests and rabbis had stood up in Jerusalem and said, "Folks, it's as plain as the Romans on our streets: This Carpenter from Nazareth really is who He claims to be. We worship You, O God!"

But ever since Lucifer himself walked the streets of heaven, some created beings would rather go down in flames doing wrong than admit to the error of their ways.

The most insidious effect of the Stockholm syndrome was that it created the illusion that something extremely dangerous seemed perfectly safe. The victims forgot what's wrong and what's right.

What does God call for? "The sacrifices of God are a broken spirit; a broken and contrite heart" (Psalm 51:17, NIV). Job uttered in Job 13:23, "How many wrongs and sins have I commmited? Show me my offense and my sin" (NIV). Even the thief on the cross who insulted Jesus couldn't get away with the plain facts. The other thief "rebuked him. 'Don't you fear God,' he said, 'since you are under the same sentence? We are punished justly, for we are getting what our deeds deserve'" (Luke 23:40, 41, NIV).

"The warfare against self is the greatest battle that was ever fought. The yielding of self, surrendering all to the will of God, requires a struggle; but the soul must submit to God before it can be renewed in holiness" (*Steps to Christ*, p. 43).

In the punchline of one *Calvin and Hobbes* comic strip (my favorite), Calvin tells his stuffed tiger, Hobbes, "Don't ever blame yourself until you've exhausted all other possibilities." We might forgive Calvin because he is a little boy, but we, the children of God, can't be forgiven for shifting the weight of what sin has done onto God and away from ourselves. If you think it's all God's fault, then Stockholm's got you.

"If we claim to be without sin, we deceive ourselves and the truth is not in us. If we confess our sins, he is faithful and just and will forgive us our sins and purify us from all unrighteousness" (1 John 1:8, 9, NIV). "Wash your hands, you sinners, and purify your hearts, you double-minded" (James 4:8, NIV). "Humble yourselves before the Lord, and he will lift you up" (verse 10, NIV).

Shaken, my police officer friend and I got into the patrol car. Wiping a smear from his cheek, he stared straight ahead. "I only came to help her," he said, starting the engine. "I just can't believe she slapped the one who came to help."

He's right. It *is* hard to believe.

BEHIND THE BACKSTOP
Andy Nash

I swung the bat as hard as I could. Then I swung it as hard as I could again. This was it. I was an Astro now, and I needed to fine-tune my swing so I could hit a home run.

I stepped up to the plate and gazed out at the pitcher. He was big—probably 8 years old. Maybe 9. And he could throw the ball hard. I'd watched him throw to our first eight hitters. *Man, did he throw hard.* Was I up to this? Was I ready for Little League?

"Go, Andy! Get a hit!" Someone seemed to think so. I turned around, panned the small crowd, and found my number one fan: Mom. She was leaning forward in her lawn chair behind the backstop. "You can do it, Andy! Whoo-oooo!"

Behind her stood Dad. He didn't say anything, but he smiled and raised his eyebrows twice. That meant he hoped I'd get a hit, but if I didn't, no big deal.

I tried my best not to smile at them, because that wouldn't be cool. But I did. I couldn't help it. I was glad they were there.

Turning again to the pitcher, I raised my bat like Rod Carew. I was ready. The pitcher leaned forward to look for an imaginary sign, then reared back, his face contorted. The ball spun off his hand and shot toward home plate. Except that it didn't go to home plate. It headed straight at me! I reeled to the right to protect my face, leaving my back exposed.

Whomp! Confusion. Pain between my shoulder blades. Tears in my eyes.

Bewildered, I thought, *Have I done something wrong? Am I out?* In desperation I turned to the blurs on the sidelines. One of the blurs had her hands over her eyes. The other blur clapped twice. "Shake it off, pal," said the blur. "Get on down to first."

I did. I got on down to first. As fast as I could run.

Getting beaned on the back by a baseball wasn't the kind of glorious beginning to Little League I'd had in mind, but it certainly was an educating one. That pitch and those that followed taught me that in baseball

THE RIDE OF YOUR LIFE

I couldn't count on much. I couldn't always count on getting a hit or catching the fly or throwing strikes.

I could count on one thing—Mom and Dad would be there. My parents didn't come to the park because my games were always exciting to watch. Fourteen consecutive walks gets dull. Nor did they come because their son played the best ball on the team. He didn't. He was the one walking 14 consecutive batters. They came for one simple reason: because they knew their attendance meant a lot to me. No matter how well or how poorly I played, I knew that Mom and Dad would encourage me from their lawn chairs behind the backstop. And *behind the backstop* was right where I needed them.

Some kids' parents didn't stay behind the backstop. Some parents sat with their children on the bench, telling them what they had done wrong last inning. Some warmed up with their children in the batter's box. Some ran the base paths and slid into home with their children. Others played the outfield with their children; some even brought their own mitts.

I felt sorry for these kids. They didn't need their parents to *play* the game for them; they just needed their parents to *be* there for them.

Luckily for me, mine were—game after game—sitting behind the backstop, following my every move, helping me when I asked for it, wincing when I did something wrong, and cheering their heads off when I got it right. I guess they figured that since I was the one wearing the size 6 Astro T-shirt, it was my game to play.

The way my parents acted at my childhood ball games (and track meets and band concerts) taught me something about support. Often the best support is the most unobtrusive support—a balance between being there for the team and staying out of the team's way.

It seems to me that the church could use a little more "backstop" support. Like a baseball team, the church can place only so many "players"— pastors, administrators, committee members—on the field at one time. These people have been charged with playing the game—with devising a strategy, making the tough decisions, leading the team to victory. Yet what happens when a problem arises? We members scramble onto the field—to the bench, to the batter's box, to the pitching mound—and try to "help" our team find a solution. We write letters, we write books, we fill Adventists On-line with 101 ways we could do things better.

But often our leaders need a different kind of help. If we were to poll our local pastors, for example, and ask them what they most needed from their congregations, what do you think they would say? More critiques?

More second-guessing? More advice? I doubt it. What our leaders often need from us the most is a simple vote of confidence, a quiet "we're with you," a show of hands. Our leaders need our support, but they need the kind of support that gives them a little room to work. They need us to pull for them with all our hearts—from behind the backstop.

Because not everyone can wear the uniform. And not everyone can play the game. But everyone can "root, root, root for the home team."

"And to self-control, perseverance . . ."

Risk!
Alex Bryan

"Whoever does not take up the cross and follow me is not worthy of me. Those who find their life will lose it, and those who lose their life for my sake will find it" (Matthew 10:38, 39, NRSV).

Gymnastics meant everything in my Adventist academy, at least to those (like me) who considered themselves gymnasts first and students second. Two-hour practices, four days a week. Long weekend tours. Countless push-ups, sit-ups, and other inspiring exercises *recommended* by our coaches. Stretching and pulling muscles. Stressing, and breaking, bones. Hours of commitment and practice, sweat and pain. The gymnastics life was demanding.

I saw the benefits of gymnastic team participation clearly: a healthy body, a good work ethic, teamwork, friendship, and cutting classes for gymnastic trips. The first four I learned to appreciate over time. The fifth I prized from the start.

A sixth benefit I've acknowledged only recently is risk. My parents understood the risk aspect the first time I stepped (or fell) on the gymnastics mats. The *value* of it didn't dawn on me for a while.

At five feet seven and 140 pounds, I've earned the right from my heredity to be at or near the top of large human pyramids. The job required a willingness to explore the virtue of risk. My efforts to perfect a reliable handstand at the top provided great opportunity. Pressing up into a handstand on top of gymnast on top of gymnast on top of gymnast on top of gymnast on top of gymnast (I'll quit before I exaggerate), I explored high altitudes nearly every day of my academy life. I threw wooden blocks out from beneath me while on my hands. I flipped backward and forward. I did things that required the removal of tiles from the gym ceiling.

It was easy then. Two broken legs didn't faze me. My brother's shattered knee couldn't stop him. My best friend has only one kidney. He wasn't allowed to play tackle football. This was no consideration in stacking six or seven people on top of him in gymnastics. Broken arms, broken collar bones, twisted body parts, near misses, crashes to the floor, and mid-air collisions struck fear in none of us.

I'm so glad I've grown up. I'd never take such risks again. How foolish.

Was it really *foolish*, though? Risk is the key ingredient in many profitable ventures. Bill Gates with risky ideas became Mr. Microsoft. Bill Clinton with political and personal risk became President Clinton. American colonists who risked their lives and their fortunes founded the United States of America. You landed your first job by taking some risk.

When Jesus says that whoever saves their life will lose it, and whoever loses their life for His sake will save it, He's talking about high-stakes risk. He's talking about taking up one's cross to follow Him, and taking up one's cross means risking it all. Christ says today, *Be a risk-taker for Me.*

Gymnastics risk I can understand. Business risks make sense in a capitalistic world. Power seems worth the price of personal failure. Risking all for Christ is another matter. What does it mean? And who will do it?

Our church has sound theology and correct application; it also maintains unity and employs the latest high-tech innovations. And Seventh-day Adventism has a huge worldwide structure. But all of these cannot substitute for risk—a trait I fear we left with our risk-taking founders many years ago.

I'm not saying risk-taking is dead in our church. There are always those who bear a cross for God. But I fear that as a people we have lost the collective desire to take chances. We're getting better at innovation—using the cutting-edge technique or the latest great idea. But risk involves much more.

The seventh-day Sabbath is sound theology, and observing this day by abstaining from work and going to church is correct application. But Sabbath observance in North America hardly requires risk. Not watching that football game or attending a Friday night concert cannot qualify as bearing one's cross. For most of us Sabbathkeeping demands no sacrifice.

Twice a decade members gather for exciting General Conference sessions. Each week we share the same Sabbath school lesson across the continent. We support world missions financially. But maintaining these aspects of our religious culture demands little sacrifice.

Our church has become involved in innovative television evangelism. The vegetarian cooking that we teach is catching on these days. We make stands against the abuse of alcohol, tobacco, and other drugs. Our leaders consistently oppose unhealthy church/state relations. But supporting these programs and issues requires little sacrifice on our part.

Not that relatively safe activities have no value. But I can believe in and support all these things with little demand on myself. My life is not in jeopardy because I subscribe to the *Adventist Review* or because I worship God publicly. My Adventist Christian aspirations do not place me under threat in America right now.

So what does being a risk-taker for God mean in a society that allows the free expression of religion? Are there no risks to take until "the end of time"?

If you want a real risk, take on the mandate of the Giraffe Society, a growing organization of Adventists who "stick their necks out for youth and young adults."* Invest wild amounts of money in your youth program. Stand up and demand that more young people be included on your church board, your conference executive committee, and as delegates to the constituency and General Conference sessions.

If you're ready for risks, defend the Christian music, drama, and other worship forms young people find meaningful—even if they're forms you don't find beneficial in your own life. Hang out with teenagers. Listen to them. Bring an earring-adorned, rock-and-roll-T-shirt-clad 15-year-old to church with you. Invite a troubled kid out to Taco Bell.

Another risk to try: downsizing your lifestyle for God. Live on less so you can give more to further His work. Can a person making $500,000 a year live on $100,000? Can a person making $80,000 a year live on $40,000? Can a person making $40,000 live on $25,000? Trade Christmas presents in for a church gift. Skip a vacation for a mission trip. Instead of trading in that car, give it to someone who has no transportation.

If you want a real risk, try *personal* evangelism. What risks will you take to save the lost? Is it too much to play golf with nonbelievers instead of believing friends to provide opportunities to introduce Christ? Is it too much to devote one night a week to dinner with an unchurched couple? Is it too much to give up the comfort of "the church family" by inviting new people into its fellowship? Is it too much to change the way you do church to make those invited feel more comfortable? Is devoting time and money to projects and forfeiting the right to one's own tastes in church worship too much risk for the Great Commission?

Would you risk becoming a missionary in another country? Would you risk spending a year working in the inner city? Would you risk moving from an Adventist community to a secular community to increase your impact on unbelievers?

When was the last time you took a kingdom risk? When did you last take a personal venture in faith? The old adage remains true: "Nothing ventured, nothing gained." We must become a risk-taking church again. Our teen and twentysomething founding fathers and mothers began a spiritual movement, and we are members of that same movement. What chances will I take for God? What chances will you take?

---

* The Giraffe Society is based at the Center for Youth Evangelism, Andrews University, Berrien Springs, Michigan. For more information, call 1-800-YOUTH2U.

Ski Lessons
A n d y   N a s h

"When they had slaughtered the bull, they brought the boy to Eli" (1 Samuel 1:25, NIV).

For the first time in my life I know what it's like to feel old. After 24 years of listening to my parents and my grandparents and all their friends moan and groan about "things not working like they used to," I finally got a taste of what they're talking about.

Not that I wanted one.

It was one Saturday night in Berrien Springs, Michigan, and Cindy and I had just returned from our first attempt at cross-country skiing at a nearby nature reserve called Love Creek, which offers night skiing on torch-lit trails.

Night skiing at Love Creek on torch-lit trails. Sounds delightful, doesn't it? That's what I thought too. Until about the eighth torch-lit hill. Then *delightful* quickly lost its charms.

As Cindy and I arrived at Love Creek that evening I felt like my usual ready-for-anything 24-year-old self. I boldly snapped on my skis, dug hard with my poles, and hauled down the first hill, brimming with determination to learn this new sport. Even after I wiped out four times in the first five minutes, I wasn't fazed. A quick bob to my feet and I was ready for more. With enough raw effort, I would soon catch on to the art of cross-country skiing.

But, to my chagrin, I wasn't catching on. Time after time I lost my balance, wobbled like a cheap tabletop, and dropped into the snow. *This is becoming less and less fun,* I mumbled to myself. My problem? Too much confidence, too little technique.

Seeing me sprawled in the snow, Cindy, who had used a NordicTrack exercise machine before, decided to risk making a few suggestions. She advised me to lift my heels when I pushed off. I thought that sounded like a ridiculous idea; after all, I didn't lift my heels in downhill skiing. Cindy also said that I would find it easier going if I kept my skis in the tracks already made on the trail. *What?* I thought. *Ski in someone else's tracks? No, I think I'll make my own tracks, thank you very much.*

After all, I figured, *I'm still young. I have all the energy in the world.*

Twenty minutes and three mild slopes later I was gasping for air like a prize-fighter in the fifteenth round. I had never tired like this as a kid. I could run on the playground forever without stopping. But at that moment I felt like a 75-year-old who needed to take a long nap.

Cindy, on the other hand, seemed to be doing just fine. Sure, she took an occasional spill (one of them was pretty hilarious, but I would never tell her that), but she hadn't fatigued half as much as I had. I resorted to pretending I was Ben-Hur in a chariot race just to keep up with her. (Males do this sort of thing.) While she was saying something about scenic beauty on a cool winter night, I was searching for the trail sign that said "This way back to the lodge."

To get back to the lodge at all, I was forced to take Cindy's counsel on skiing technique. To my surprise, it worked. Lifting my heels off my skis kept me balanced and moving forward easily. And keeping my skis in the smooth grooves already on the trail allowed me to glide along instead of plowing like a moose through the untracked snow.

Unfortunately, I accepted these ideas just as my energy ran out, which *really* frustrated me. By the time I learned the secrets of skiing, my arms and legs had called it quits. The smarter I got, the slower I got. If only I could have put my energy and my wisdom together. Then I would have skied well.

Such is the tension between young Adventists and older Adventists. As young upstarts with no training or old pros with no stamina, we both want to run the church our own way.

Say the young Adventists: "We should run the church because we're the ones with all the energy, determination, and creativity. Sure, we may not understand everything about the church and its history, but hand us a set of skis and poles, and we'll figure it out as we blaze our own path."

Say the older Adventists: "We should run the church because we're the ones with all the experience, wisdom, and common sense. True, we may not have the physical endurance we used to have, but we know the best way through the woods, and eventually we'll make it home."

So who has the better case? Energy or experience? Neither, of course.

❀ ❀ ❀

"The boy Samuel ministered before the Lord under Eli. In those days the word of the Lord was rare; there were not many visions.

"One night Eli, whose eyes were becoming so weak that he could barely see, was lying down in his usual place. The lamp of God had not yet gone out, and Samuel was lying down in the temple of the Lord, where the ark of God was. Then the Lord called Samuel.

"Samuel answered, 'Here I am.' And he ran to Eli and said, 'Here I am; you called me.'

"But Eli said, 'I did not call; go back and lie down.' So he went and lay down" (1 Samuel 3:1-5, NIV).

The Seventh-day Adventist Church cannot be run solely by Samuels. Like first-time skiers, we would consume all our energy and determination learning the system—which techniques work and which don't; how to recognize God's voice; and how not to be fooled by the devil's tricks. Furthermore, we can't possibly reach the older generations the way our elders can. How could we identify with the Depression and World War II and Vietnam? Thinking we're ready to run our church alone is a sure sign we still have plenty of maturing to do.

Just as Samuel ran to Eli, we young Adventists must run to our elders with questions and frustrations and ideas. And we must listen to them so that we don't repeat the mistakes they learned from. We must build on what our elders know. Let me illustrate.

I loved circuses while I was growing up. Big circuses, small circuses—I didn't care. I loved them all. So it stood to reason that when I (a 7-year-old) saw in the *TV Guide* a show promising not just a circus but a flying circus, I should beg to stay up two hours past my bedtime and watch it. Even after my mom and dad said that I probably wouldn't enjoy *Monty Python's Flying Circus* very much, I insisted vehemently that yes, I would enjoy it very much, so could I please watch it, please, please. My parents smiled at each other and obliged.

Ten o'clock came, and I sat at the TV, ready to watch the greatest show on earth. By 10:05 I was mildly perplexed. By 10:10 I was in bed. They were right: *Monty Python's Flying Circus* had been a major disappointment. (For those of you lucky enough to be ignorant, *Monty Python* is a strange British comedy that has nothing to do with a circus.)

"Listen, my sons, to a father's instruction; pay attention and gain understanding. I give you sound learning, so do not forsake my teaching" (Proverbs 4:1, 2, NIV).

In January 1994 the Southern College newspaper asked students this poll question: "What is your impression of our church leaders at the General Conference?" Forty-nine percent said they had a "favorable" impression; 16

percent said their impression was "unfavorable"; and 35 percent weren't sure.

In response to the poll, Adventist Intercollegiate Association president Krisi Clark said she was worried about the third who had no opinion. "Our students don't have a clue what's going on up there," she said, "and we have a vested interest."

I agree. We need to get a clue before we criticize. We need to take an interest before we take to bemoaning. We need to check in with our church leaders before we chastise their choices. We need to leaf through the *Review* and *Ministry* and *Liberty* before we launch our own magazines. We need to attend church business meetings before we complain we're not GC delegates. We need to do these things before we insist we can run the church better. Otherwise, we won't be helping at all.

❋ ❋ ❋

"Again the Lord called, 'Samuel!' And Samuel got up and went to Eli and said, 'Here I am; you called me.'

" 'My son,' Eli said, 'I did not call; go back and lie down.'

"Now Samuel did not yet know the Lord: The word of the Lord had not yet been revealed to him" (1 Samuel 3:6, 7, NIV).

But neither can this church be run solely by Elis. Like retired Olympic skiers whose days have come and gone, older Adventists no longer have the energy and determination to compete. Experience alone is not enough; you must also have the vigor of youth to lead the church into the next century just as those with youthful vigor led us into this century. And speaking of youth, many of the old methods no longer reach young people as they once did. It's no one's fault; that's just the way it is.

But that doesn't mean you older Adventists can't teach us anything. When we, like Samuel, run to you in the night and tell you that we hear a call, don't send us away. Don't tell us to keep quiet, to go back to our rooms and lie down. Instead, listen to our questions and concerns. Listen to our dreams and remember when you used to wake up at night with dreams of your own. If our ideas are wrong, don't just tell us they're wrong. Show us how we can make them right. Let us learn from your mistakes and, when you think we're ready, let us lead.

"Train a child in the way he should go, and when he is old he will not turn from it" (Proverbs 22:6, NIV).

During the summer of 1992 I worked as an intern with the *Adventist Review* at the General Conference headquarters. Each of my 10 weeks there I spent time with a different editor. My day-to-day interaction with the *Review* staff—sitting in on their meetings, noting their editorial decisions, watching them handle criticism, witnessing their prayers—was more valuable to me than any textbook or journalism class ever could be.

One afternoon at the GC I met *Liberty* editor Clifford Goldstein. I told Clifford that I was interning with the *Review* and learning a lot, and he replied that that reminded him of his own experience with the previous editor of *Liberty*, Roland Hegstad.

"Hegstad was hard on me," Clifford said, "and I took a beating continually for 10 years, but I loved every minute because I knew he was making me better." Clifford said that he would also be interested in having a summer intern work with him—not to beat on continually, I assume, but to train.

Makes a lot of sense, doesn't it? I wonder how many other Adventist leaders, and not just pastors, would also welcome a young intern for a summer or for a year. As Samuel "ministered before the Lord under Eli," so could hundreds of our most energetic young Adventists learn from our wisest older Adventists. We need to do something. Because not until our thousands of Elis and thousands of Samuels put their efforts together will our church ski through the woods quickly on a torch-lit trail. That has to be our goal.

"The Lord called Samuel a third time, and Samuel got up and went to Eli and said, 'Here I am; you called me.'

"Then Eli realized that the Lord was calling the boy. So Eli told Samuel, 'Go and lie down, and if he calls you, say, "Speak, Lord, for your servant is listening."' So Samuel went and lay down in his place.

"The Lord came and stood there, calling as at the other times, 'Samuel! Samuel!'

"Then Samuel said, 'Speak, for your servant is listening'" (1 Samuel 3:8-10, NIV).

For an old man named Eli and a young man named Samuel, the formula was remarkably simple: a little communication, a little cooperation, a little humility. And the result remarkably big: the voice of God.

Who's to say the same couldn't happen today?

"And to self-control, perseverance . . ."

My Mother Tried to Kill Me
Victor Czerkasij

With two healthy sons aged 5 and 7, you try to keep your bases covered and always have something for them to do, or that old dictum will surely come to pass: *The devil finds work for idle hands.* Unfortunately for my mother, living on the fourth floor of a Brooklyn brownstone in 1968, competition with the devil was too close to call. My younger brother Jerry and I could find little to do on rainy days.

Jerry, incidentally, is not my brother's legal name. He was christened Yaroslav, after a very wise king from ancient Ukrainian history. The kids at school would tease Jerry and call him "You're-a-slob," which, on the face of it, is very funny. Unless you're Yaroslav.

Anyway, to pass the time, we would slip on Father's thick, white cotton work socks and take off running from the bedroom. We'd achieve maximum speed in a short corridor that served as the kitchen and burst out into the living room. The glory in all this was skating across the most freshly waxed, slippery wooden floor in the five boroughs of New York. Our imaginations had fixed on the far wall as the "crash site," designed to stop out-of-control formula one Grand Prix Indy 500 racecars, of which there were two.

My mom then became de facto race official, wildly waving her dishcloth like a checkered flag and telling us to *slow down or someone's going to get hurt.* Oh, sure. Like Al Unser won races by listening to his mother.

One of the laws of the universe assures mothers that they will be proved right eventually. Sort of a cosmic "I told you so." I received my wake-up call in the straightaway when my right heel hit the point of a large, cleverly angled splinter as I neared the crash site. Al Unser never faced this at the Brickyard.

Mom flew into action as I flew into a frenzy. Grabbing me around the waist, she yanked the reddening sock off my foot to assess the damage. The splinter had snapped off deep, and she couldn't pinch it with her nails. She needed a precise surgical tool and found salad tongs. The probing began.

THE RIDE OF YOUR LIFE

Our landlady, Mrs. Gianelli, already regretted renting the upstairs apartment to a young couple with two hellions. She should have advertised "Pets Welcome, but No Children!" Her usual way of commenting on our behavior was to glare. She would bang on the ceiling with a broom handle during race days. Later, in college psychology classes, I identified Mrs. Gianelli as a passive-aggressive and borderline nervous breakdown.

But the screaming over the splinter broke the broom handle's back, so to speak. Mrs. Gianelli stomped up the stairs and flung open the apartment door. What greeted her eyes was a scene for the police files: a mother determinedly gouging her 7-year-old son's heel with salad tongs and giving him a very good chance for the best dramatic performance Oscar. The other son, in his supporting role, whimpering as he sits on the floor, holding a bloodied sock. Mrs. Gianelli might have been in her 80s, but she knew child abuse when she saw it.

Screaming in Sicilian, she called her three sons, who had wisely chosen to live on the first floor. These young men, who without a doubt were to play bit parts in *The Godfather*, approached my obviously deranged mother with the intent to protect me from her. They didn't account, however, for the power of a loaded pair of salad tongs.

Waving the kitchen implement in front of them, Mom quickly explained the situation to the men, who whispered a calm translation to our badly frightened landlady. Much to my horror, one of the sons then offered to *help my mother with my foot*. Within seconds I was immobilized by people who ate too much pasta, and remained that way until the splinter saw the light of day.

Poor Mrs. Gianelli. The view that had greeted her was only half the story. I suppose that you could headline what she first saw as: "Mother Hurts Son." After learning a little more, she could say, "Mother Rescues Son."

Have we treated God this way? Have you ever asked Him point-blank in your prayers, "What are You doing? This really hurts in ways I'm not sure You fully appreciate. From all that I can gather, Your planning goes against all reason and common sense. Please, Lord, let's do it the way *I* want."

Suppose I had asked God to save me from my mother the time I caught the splinter. It would have festered in my foot and hurt much more. You can't go through life with a splinter the size of the Washington Monument in your right heel even if your prayer is to leave it alone. I now realize it was for the best that the Provolone Brothers sat on me.

I learned that God *does* understand. In fact, the tables have turned over the years, and now I am the one trying to understand *Him* rather than wishing He would consider my point of view. I'm trying to grasp how Jesus willingly chose to die for me, to love me unto *death* despite knowing that I might choose to reject Him. I want to understand how He placed His trust in His Father while hanging on the cross, rejected by humanity and seemingly left alone by God. All He saw was the tomb looming before Him. Not resurrection, but separation from the ones He had always loved.

No splinters in His heel, but thick nails that His mother longed to remove. "He doesn't understand," you say? God's forte is to go against what we consider logical and bring us to the perspective of living as He knows best. " 'For my thoughts are not your thoughts, neither are your ways my ways,' declares the Lord. 'As the heavens are higher than the earth, so are my ways higher than your ways and my thoughts than your thoughts'"(Isaiah 55:8, 9, NIV).

My own son recently took up the sport of grabbing bugs. Any kind—beetles and crickets, grasshoppers and butterflies, bees and wasps. I wish he would listen to me when I tell him he could get hurt. After all, doesn't he know that a father knows best?

"And to self-control, perseverance . . ."

THE ONLY OPINION THAT COUNTS
Alex Bryan

I hold opinions on lots of things. I think Breyer's mint chocolate chip is the king of ice creams. I think we need stricter gun-control laws. I think baseball is the best of all sports. I think contemporary Christian music is pretty good stuff. I think my mom is the greatest. I think bow ties are cool. I have strong opinions about abortion, women's ordination, and Newt Gingrich, too.

Opinions are important. Without them we would be in bad shape. Together our opinions establish societies, trends, entertainment, and legal precedents. Without them we would accomplish little.

We nurture relationships with opinions. "No, dear, I don't care where we go, what we eat, and whether you wear a tie or dirty T-shirt." That would get very blah really fast. We appreciate the nuances of our religion with opinions. "Does it matter if I believe in God or not? Does it matter if I swear at you? Does it matter if I steal your car?" If you answer, "No, it doesn't matter; I have no opinions," you also lack values.

God even wants you to form opinions about *Him*. The great controversy boils down to your opinion, your assessment, about God. Satan says your opinion should be negative. Jesus says your opinion should be positive. In the judgment your opinion about Jesus is the central issue. Is the cross foolishness or an act of love and salvation?

But this is where God wants our opinions to stop. We can make judgments about issues on earth. We must make judgments about God and His Word. But *the* judgment belongs to Him. We must keep out of it. Only one opinion counts—and it ain't mine or yours.

The judgment conjures up scary thoughts for many. Am I good enough? Did I ask forgiveness for *every* sin? What if I . . . ? I worry about it because my life isn't so wonderful.

Here's the good news: The judgment is *great* news. Christ, as our advocate, covers for us. He lived a sinless life. He is everything we need to be. And He acts as our judge too. No one judges us but the One who loves us. No one's opinion matters except that of the One who thinks we're incredible.

Jesus' decision is clear: We should spend eternity in heaven. The pre-Advent judgment remains His alone. It's an event to love, not fear. As long as I don't come to the unthinkable conclusion that the cross is foolishness, I'm in. Period.

That's *His* opinion. Yeah, God!

GIVE GOD A HAND
Victor Czerkasij

*A*ll Adventists, it seems, have a personal horror story about a fellow church member. Just as someone at the retirement center mentioning what ails them raises an uproar in the whole wing, so Adventists will launch into debates over who has the worst scar or who came to the most harm and get everyone riled up. For some, the event stays with them as an unforgettable, unforgivable encounter.

I was not born into this denomination, and I had the opportunity to choose my walk. Many of my friends feel they had their religious heritage thrust on them. When my family joined the church, we were like salmon shooting up the rapids, trying to make our way to quieter streams. But so many were heading out. Why?

One source of disgruntlement, especially for those born into Adventist families, is the greener pastures you think you see outside the church. I grew up in the Ukrainian Greek Orthodox Church. The sanctuaries contain no pews because, Orthodox believe, it would be an affront to God to *sit* in His presence. Visiting my first SDA church, I was pretty amazed that I would not have to stand for three hours in a closed room with burning candles sucking the oxygen from my brain. And no cold cross to kiss after a hundred other members had had their turn. I *did* miss whipping the sins from fellow parishioners by means of pussy willow boughs during a traditional Easter service, but I found that what goes around comes around.

Thankful in my new Adventist world, I was not prepared for my new friends' complaints. *We have to stand for hymns, kneel for prayer. The preacher is so boring. The old people stare. I'm not allowed to go shopping today. I can't eat lobster. I can't drink coffee.*

And here I was, hearing for the first time that Jesus Christ is actually God in the flesh. That He came to show me a better way. That He will return to take me home. And that heaven can begin right here and now (it's been like heaven to me just to sit down).

I was thinking, *How can I repay You, Lord? What can I do to make You happy?* All my friends knew the commandments, but so many remained untouched by the Commandment-giver.

I taught tenth-grade Bible in an Adventist school. Not in the usual setup, though, because the majority of students at *this* school were not Seventh-day Adventists. Among more than 20 students in class that day, only *one* was of the (cliché alert) *remnant church*. He was dozing in the back row. Mormons made up a bloc off to the right, while the Presbyterians and Episcopalians sat, naturally, to the left. My few Baptists and a lone Buddhist met square in the center.

The lesson that day detailed the Sabbath doctrine. I could feel the breath of the Holy Spirit as my students, eyes wide and mouths quiet, scribbled my every verse and comment as I presented (cliché alert) *this present truth*.

I sensed that some pastors and parents would be bombarded with questions like the ones arising in class: "This is great, but what do we do? Will God hold us accountable if we know the truth and still go to church on Sunday? Would you like to speak to my priest?" Clearly I had reached a defining moment in my teaching career and these students' lives.

The devil knew it too. He must have decided it was time to wake someone up, if just for a moment.

"The Sabbath stinks!" he bleated. (To be honest, I have removed the actual terminology he used.) Every head jerked around as the lone Adventist student heaped a torrent of abuse on the fourth commandment. I suppose I could have lunged out and escorted him from the room, but everyone else would have wondered what I was hiding.

So I let him spout a minute more, then I gave them the usual blather that we can "disagree but not be disagreeable."

But it was too late. The damage could not be undone. He flopped his head back on the desktop, satisfied, looking for all the world like a discarded toy that a puppeteer had tired of.

It had been the usual litany of grievances, and it began with the words "I can't . . ." Because young people think of their friends as founts of wisdom, the rest of the class stared at me as if to say "Traitor. You almost had us. We nearly fell for it. Good thing we were rescued by a true voice from the inside."

Would it make sense for Satan to drive *everyone* out of the church? Isn't it to his advantage to keep a certain few in the pews who can do the job for him from the inside?

The Ride of Your Life

A converted Seventh-day Adventist who knows the truth is a marvelous work to behold, much like a fine clock: open face, faithful hands, and good works. But a Seventh-day Adventist who knows *only* the facts and not a love for God is a loose cannon on the ship of faith. What is more dangerous, an enemy or an ally with no sense of allegiance?

When my mom was baptized in the early seventies, she faithfully took my brother, my sister, and me with her to church. The small Peekskill, New York, SDA Church made up in fervor what it lacked in space. Folk sat shoulder to shoulder, close enough to peer over at your *Guide* magazine and read with you.

Vineyard Voices was a popular feature each week. Right after the lesson study, people could stand right where they were and share (as they were often reminded) their *"short* testimony to the Lord."

Mom never heard the word "short." But she knew "testimony." Walking into church late on any given Sabbath, you would have thought that the sermon was being given by a woman from near the front pew on the right.

My brother Jerry and I reacted as most 13-year-olds would. We glanced at each other, rolled our eyes, and slid our heels slowly under the pew in front of us, dragging our bodies down until you thought that two vertically challenged people were worshiping with the congregation that day.

One day someone tapped us on the shoulders, and we looked up. A longtime member of the church had noticed our discomfort and, supposing to help, whispered hoarsely, "Don't worry. One day she'll cool off."

Mom never did, but the shoulder tapper called it quits after a while.

I'm staying. I'm staying because I'm in love.

BRANCHES
Alex Bryan

*H*ave you ever had to introduce yourself and explain who you are?

"Hello, my name is Alex, and I'm . . ."

What should I say? Do I tell them where I work? where I'm from? who my parents are? where I graduated from college? about my hobbies and recreational interests? about my life passions? who my most famous friend is?

How should I describe myself to someone who does not know me?

I suppose it might depend on whom I'm being introduced to. To a professional or someone accomplished in academia, perhaps I should describe my college experience. To an older person, maybe I should ask whether they know my grandparents. If it's someone from far away, I might talk about my hometown—the weather, geography, tax rates, per-capita crime rate, etc. Selling products for fund-raisers when I was growing up, I always introduced myself, "Hello, I'm Dr. Bryan's son, Alex," as if my relationship to my father the physician would somehow enhance my credibility as a salesman.

I took two majors in college—theology and history. The theology major, of course, stuck me with a certain label: "Those future pastors, they're all on a hunt to find a wife!" I often identified myself as a history major for greater safety in the dating arena.

Who we are is not only elaborate and complicated; it's also very important to us. Knowing my identity—what gives me my place in this world, what makes me unique, what makes me comfortable in relation to the rest of the world—and the universe, for that matter—is crucial.

We don't think about discovering identity every day. But unconsciously we search for what will secure and shape our lives all the time.

Christianity provides a unique opportunity to discover identity. Jesus helps us with these words: "I am the vine; *you are the branches*" (John 15:5, NIV). According to Christ, we are branches.

Branches stay attached to a tree while they are alive. They are rooted to something. The wind blows, the seasons change—and the branch grows. New branches grow from the trunk. One thing remains constant: Life flows from the trunk to the branch.

Christians remain attached to Jesus no matter what changes come along. As creations of the Maker, as saved children of the Redeemer, as citizens of the heavenly kingdom of God, we are not lost in the confused secular theories of humanity's place in the universe. Christians know for sure that they are related to God.

Why does this matter? Car accidents, plane crashes, train wrecks, earthquakes, tornadoes, hurricanes, cancer, AIDS—all the catastrophes of this world—are devastating to a person devoid of identity-source security. My generation—the twentysomethings—enter the adult world with dismal prospects for the decades to come. Happy days are not here again. Problems mount faster than solutions. Fear will eventually kill my generation. Knowing my Source *matters very much.*

"The only answer is Jesus." If you grew up going to Sabbath school, you heard it until the phrase became a cliché. But only strong identity-source security can control twenty-first-century fear. Jesus *is* the answer in our volatile world. Only the consistency of God underlies our shaky existence as an immovable foundation. Yes, it's not *what* you know, but *who* you know that will get you through.

Although they are all attached to the tree, branches also differ from one another. And they perform different functions.

Some branches house bird nests.

Some branches provide shade on a hot day.

Some branches, like those on a dogwood, bear beautiful flowers.

Some branches support a tree house.

Some branches hold swings.

Some branches bear fresh green leaves.

Some branches allow moss to cover them.

Some branches provide stomping grounds for squirrels.

Some branches produce delicious fruit or nuts.

Some branches are big; some branches are small; some branches are high; some branches are low.

Not all branches serve all purposes. Some branches support my weight. Some don't. Some branches provide shade. Some don't. I wouldn't eat the produce off a pine tree, but I would from an apple tree. Each branch serves a unique function.

Paul refers to the functions of individual Christians as spiritual gifts.

He explains that we receive gifts by location, by opportunity, and by design. We are made and placed for a purpose. The key for each Christian is to discover their unique place on the tree.

If the Coca-Cola Company were a Christian organization, it would offer a fine example of understanding one's gift. I visited the Coca-Cola museum in Atlanta, Georgia, and found a company that knows its identity. Those who run the company know their niche, and Coca-Cola is a blue-chip company because of it.

I watched videos that teach the museum-goer about the rich history of Coca-Cola. I listened to museum employees, sharply dressed in Coca-Cola red, answer with eagerness every question asked about the product. I watched all the old Coke commercials. I heard a recorded presentation from the CEO. Tears almost welled up in my eyes as I learned of Coca-Cola's invaluable contribution to our planet. I left the museum actually excited about sugar water in an aluminum can.

You won't find Coca-Cola in the four food groups, but the Coca-Cola Company knows its identity and its mission. Successful companies are confident about what they are and what they're all about.

Christians gain confidence in their gifts the same way. Let me serve God as I preach, speak, write, lead, and discuss the future in boardrooms. But please don't make me sing, act, paint, cook, design, teach kindergarten, or pass out literature. My branch is specialized, and when I operate in the areas of my gifts, I love being a Christian. When I don't, I can't stand the Christian life.

You may hate public speaking, writing, leading, and boardrooms. Praise God—you're normal! You possess incredible gifts I can't touch because you are a very different branch.

"Who am I?" "Where do I fit in this world?" Two huge questions for Generation Xers. Jesus answers both questions in one dynamic phrase: *I am the vine; you are the branches.* I know my source, and I know my place in His world. My name is Alex and I . . .

"And to perseverance, godliness . . ."

VESSELS
Victor Czerkasij

I heard a father tell the story of a walk he and his young son took in the woods. They drove away from home together in the family van to spend some quality time. Dad hoped to show his boy the animal tracks in the snow by a wooded area not far from their home.

Pulling over to the side of the road, they got out and strode away hand-in-hand to follow the footprints of birds and deer in the white fluff.

They topped a small rise and heard a stream burbling just below. The spray from a steep drop had splashed up and frozen, creating long, thin icicles that chimed in the cold breeze.

The sun shone on father and son through the clear air, sparkling on a perfect winter's day.

Their moment of peace, however, broke with the crunch of tires on gravel. They heard the alarmed shouts of men, the slamming of car doors, and the jangling of metal on metal. Over the rise came a posse of out-of-breath police officers and sheriff's deputies.

"Freeze, mister," the lead lawman ordered, pointing at the father. In fear and confusion, the father did as he was told. But the young boy hugged his father by the leg and asked, loudly enough so all could hear, "Daddy, what do these men want?"

The officials halted in their tracks.

"Is that your *daddy*, son?" Receiving an affirming nod from the boy, the officer asked the father, "Is that your son, sir?" Finding his nerve, the father blurted, "Yes, and can you please tell me what this is about?"

Looking sheepish, the officer explained that the police department had received a call about a man leading a child into the woods. They'd been spotted "holding hands." Overall, it had looked pretty suspicious.

"Sorry, sir," one deputy said. "You just never know these days." With that, the officers walked away, leaving a sickened young father with a be-wildered child.

As ridiculous as it sounds, in today's world a father and son spending time together has become, to the casual observer, more of an aberration than the norm. The beautiful has become ugly.

That's because some things aren't what they seem.

The generation that begot the so-called baby boomers have had a tough time. Here's a whole group of people just entering Social Security age who can't figure out what went wrong with people *my* age. "That sure doesn't sound like church music from when *we* were growing up," they say.

As a boomer who rubs shoulders with Andy and Alex (two Generation Xers who I hope will be there for my Social Security), I find myself out of place. I don't catch their lingo, and I'm slow to see their vision of the church and its place in the world. Not that their point of view isn't valid, but now I'm the dinosaur, ponderously evaluating it all against my experience.

I remember Mom not letting me sing "I Want to Hold Your Hand" because the Beatles were "filthy." Today it's quaint. Times change.

Am I saying things are getting worse from generation to generation? Maybe. Didn't we have sin in past times? Yes. But we face a terrific challenge, no matter what our ages and differences: how to live pure lives in an increasingly impure world.

Today headlines arise when someone simply dares to question the acceptance of what is now standard practice. In Fort Lauderdale, Florida, the local newspaper ran the headline "Parents Protest Nude Doughnut Shop." The angle of the article, as I remember, made the parents look like intolerant kooks. "'They're just bigots,' customers fumed." It's a truly amazing feat for a society: Behavior that was once considered desirable has become irrelevant. Meanwhile, the strange and bizarre take the driver's seat.

You remember the party that had probably been going on for quite a while. The officials alone numbered a thousand—not including spouses, lesser-knowns, hired help, and slaves.

When King Belshazzar held a banquet, he desired that it would be an affair to remember. With this party he succeeded beyond his wildest imaginings. Daniel 5:2 says that when Belshazzar was drinking wine, he ordered that the holy vessels stolen from the Temple in Jerusalem be brought to the great hall. You'd *have* to be under the influence to play with the vessels consecrated to the service of God.

Belshazzar filled these goblets, pitchers, and chalices with alcohol and sang songs to the gods of Babylon. Pictures and statues of these gods might well have stood in the hall itself, made by the hand of man from gold and silver, bronze and iron, wood and stone. Each stood lifeless and unseeing. Only in the muddled imaginations of the revelers did they come to life. But now the Universal Designated Driver was about to show His hand.

"Mene, mene, tekel upharsin" translates, very roughly, as "there comes a time when enough is enough." Human beings have always had the option to desecrate themselves and suffer the consequences someday. But by desecrating what has been dedicated to the holy God, a person crosses the line to immediate condemnation. Daniel 5:30 reports, "That same night Belshazzar the . . . king was slain" (NASB).

Remember, this was not an angry God lashing out at someone who had irritated Him. Jeremiah 51:9 records God's words: "[I] would have healed Babylon, but she would not be healed" (NEB).

There are things God cannot do. Remember forgiven sins or change His word, for example. And God cannot be different from what His Son revealed to us—perfect, holy, unchanging.

As we behold true godliness, we change. God does not.

Moses approached God at His invitation in Exodus 3. But notice that God directed Moses to take off his shoes, for the ground that he trod on was holy ground. What made it holy? Simply the presence of God.

Belshazzar's feast reminds us that as vessels set aside for the service of God, we live in the world but have no part in its impure revelry. We face a challenge as Seventh-day Adventist Christians: We must decide every day what we will place in our vessels. Will it be the sludge of gossip, pride, or lies? Maybe a coveted position or title, or merchandise at the mall? Perhaps hatred for parents or someone at church?

We identify vessels partly by what they harbor. No one shops at food stores with dirty garbage cans! The same is true of the holy vessels at the feast: They were intended only to serve the true God. They found their calling in performing the function they were intended for.

What, then, is the calling of a Seventh-day Adventist?

"And to perseverance, godliness . . ."

State-of-the-Art Car Alarms and Shirt-Pocket Telephones
Andy Nash

*Y*ou could hear her coming from a mile away. Literally.

One gorgeous spring morning during my junior year of college, I walked from my dormitory to Brock Hall for my 8:00 magazine-writing class. The day was warm, and aside from a few chattering squirrels hunting for acorns and a student sprinting back to the dorm to get the assignment he had forgotten, the campus was quiet.

Suddenly the quiet was sliced by a distant noise, an annoyingly familiar noise—a car alarm.

I had heard plenty of car alarms before—most memorably, outside my window at 2:00 in the morning and, before that, in the church parking lot during prayer. But I had never heard a car alarm that seemed to build in intensity.

It seemed as if the car alarm were . . . coming toward me. I swung to my right.

Down the road came a woman in her mid-20s, driving a light-blue Honda Civic. With car alarm blaring, she cut the car hard into the Brock Hall parking lot. Everyone within earshot (most of Hamilton County) stopped to watch. Groundsworkers leaned on their shovels, students gathered on the sidewalk, squirrels put down their acorns. The woman whipped the Civic into an empty parking space and turned off the engine. Immediately the car alarm stopped.

She shoved her door open, got out, yanked her backpack out from under the seat, and slammed the door with her foot. Stepping onto the sidewalk, she began to mumble something about state-of-the-art *junk* and something about someone named Gary.

At this point she was walking right behind me, mad as a bull. I suppose I should have left her alone, but I was a journalism student. "What's wrong with your alarm?" I asked. She shook her head slowly and said that she didn't know. She had taken it to the garage the day before, but no one knew why the alarm came on only while the car was going. Her husband, Gary, knew how to fix it, but he was out of town that week.

I remarked that she must really dread driving her car. She glared at me as if to say "Duh" and then said that, yes, she did dread driving her car, and that it was especially miserable at stoplights. I told her I was sorry and wished her luck. Later that morning I heard her drive away. I was in class at the time.

Poor woman—something designed to make her life less worrisome was doing the exact opposite.

She's not alone.

Cut to the June 6, 1994, issue of *Fortune* magazine, and hold on to your sanity, because you're living in the age of information. Writer Rick Tetzeli calls it the infobog—"a pervasive, invasive information infrastructure that is as much a part of our lives as religion was for medieval serfs."

Americans boast nearly 150 million E-mail addresses, cellular phones, pagers, fax machines, voice-mailboxes, and answering machines. "Garbage at the speed of light," says one businessman.

These items are designed to make our lives easier, but our lives aren't easier. The average U.S. executive spends six weeks a year retrieving lost information. Fifty-one percent of Americans say they don't have enough time in their days (except to watch TV—45 percent of us watch two or more hours a day).

Microchips pour out of factories faster than ever, paper production is up 53 percent from 1987, and we have more than three times more telephones on our desks and countertops than we had seven years ago.

The result? A nationwide headache. (Pain reliever sales are up $500 million since 1987.)

The infobog. Are you keeping up? Do you still have your senses? Are you about ready to slap a stamp on your modem and mail it to someone who needs it more? Are you overwhelmed by it all?

Take an aspirin. Then take heart. You're in the right church, and there is a prescription for better living.

But first let me share a prescription for better writing.

Last year I taught English composition at Andrews University. Each new quarter I told my students how I possessed one of the qualities of good writing when I was 8, and how I've been trying to get it back ever since.

The quality is simplicity, and it's really no big secret. "Keep it simple, stupid," goes the old saying. Less is more. Cut, cut, cut.

The best formula I've seen for clear, simple writing is in William Zinsser's book *On Writing Well:* "Look for clutter in your writing and prune it ruthlessly. Be grateful for everything you can throw away. Reexamine each sentence that you put on paper. Is every word doing new work? Can any thought be expressed with more economy? Is anything pompous or pretentious or faddish? Are you hanging on to something useless just because you think it's beautiful? Simplify, simplify."

At first some of my students resist this advice. They think it might ruin their writing style, which features all the big words they learned in high school. But by the end of the quarter most of them realize that it only strengthens their writing style.

Simplicity. It's a proven element of good writing.

And it's a proven element of good living.

For years the Adventist Church has said that a simple life is the best life. Drawing from Adam and Eve's lost life in Eden, Solomon's realization that much of this life is meaningless, and Jesus' admonition to the rich young ruler about the first part of his name, our church has crafted a set of standards for good living, a formula for relative peace in a raucous world.

You've heard portions of this formula all your life. Don't drink, don't smoke, don't gamble. Don't wear jewelry, don't dress like that, don't dress like that, either. Don't dance, don't watch so much television, don't listen to that kind of music. Don't worry about what others have, don't worry about what others make, don't worry about the world's definition of success.

Contrary to common belief, this formula wasn't designed to make our lives more difficult; it was designed to make our lives easier.

Now, there is nothing inherently evil about jewelry and expensive clothes, television and computer Solitaire. It's what we do with them, how we spend our time and money on them, how we let them clutter our lives, that brings problems:

- when we hook into *Time* on-line to read about infidelity rather than having dinner with our spouse;
- when we buy a Super Sega Genesis 99,000 to show our kids we love them rather than taking them sledding or caving in the world Genesis 1 describes;
- when we scour through computer magazines for the fastest, most innovative ways to call anyone in the world rather than scouring those old Scriptures in search of One not of this world.

What's the solution? Do we ignore the latest technology altogether?

Of course not. Adventists shouldn't live like Puritans or Buddhist monks any more than college writing students should write oversimplified, "See Spot bark"-type sentences. As usual, the secret is balance. When God gave Adam and Eve everything they needed to be truly happy, He didn't include an E-mail account. But neither did He include a command to lie around and stagnate. God gave us brains to help us decide which things will better our lives and which won't.

A couple years ago I attended the Adventist Intercollegiate Association convention at Union College in Lincoln, Nebraska. Each Adventist college sends about 10 student officers to these meetings so they can network with, learn from, and fall in love with student officers from other colleges.

We heard a guest speaker that weekend—a young, hip, rich business executive named Jay. For one hour Jay told us how we could be entrepreneurial and cool like him. "Be a creator of circumstance, not a creature of circumstance," Jay urged. "Be decisive, get serious, dream big dreams. Associate with success-minded people. Make a quality decision that you achieve your goals no matter what obstacles get in your way."

Jay then told us about one purchase we should plan to make: a shirt-pocket telephone.

"By 1996," Jay said, "shirt-pocket telephones will enable people to call anyone from anywhere in the world by linking directly to a new network of 77 satellites placed by Motorola. The caller will not need to know the location of the person being called. The system will automatically locate the receiver by his or her identifying number. The phones will need a power output of only half a watt and an antenna less than four inches long."

What Jay had to say about success and shirt-pocket telephones certainly made a lot of sense. For a while I even took notes. Yet something didn't seem quite right about Jay's presentation. Something was missing. Later that afternoon I realized what it was.

As I was sitting on the steps of the building in which Jay had motivated us, Chris Blake walked up. Chris had been the editor of *Insight* magazine for several years and moved on to teach at Union. I admire Chris and his talents, and I wondered why he had chosen to teach at a small college when he could have gone after more prestige and more money elsewhere, as Jay told us to do. I asked him about it.

"I'm happy here," Chris replied. "I love to teach, and I have so much more time for my family. This is what I needed."

His face supported his words. He looked so much more *content* with his unprestigious job and average salary than the rich young executive who ran his own company had looked earlier that day. And everything became crystal clear to me.

Time for God, time for family, and a good job that takes away from neither—that's the way Chris had found contentment and Jay had not. That's the kind of contentment the Adventist Church encourages. And that's the kind of contentment I want for myself. Maybe you do too.

Look for the clutter in your life and prune it ruthlessly. Be grateful for everything you can throw away. Reexamine each new toy that you put on your office desk or kitchen counter. Is it really saving time? Can you do without it? Does anything you own cut into moments with family or moments with God? Are you hanging on to something useless just because everyone else has one? Do you really need a state-of-the-art car alarm? Do you really need a shirt-pocket telephone?

Simplify, simplify.

The L Word

Alex Bryan

We show great concern for proper terminology these days.

We use "African-American," "Native American," "Latin American," and "European American" instead of less-sensitive words. Instead of "handicapped" we say a person "has a disability." We say "salesperson" and "chairperson" instead of "salesman" and "chairman." And the list goes on.

I think this is all very good—especially for the Christian community. Uplifting and respecting all people must be one of our core values. And uplifting people often starts with the things we say. Solomon said that "a wholesome tongue is a tree of life" (Proverbs 15:4). "But a harsh word stirs up anger" (verse 1, NIV).

With this in mind, I propose that we eliminate one popular yet deceptively damaging term within Christianity—and especially Adventism: laity, including all its variations—layperson, lay member, layman, lay-woman, lay activities, lay workers, lay ministries, etc.

There's so much to hate about the word *lay*. In Christian circles the word *laity* distinguishes the difference between "professional" Christians (i.e., ministers) and amateurs—those who are merely the laity.

Webster says that *laity* is "the mass of the people as distinguished from those of a particular profession or those specially skilled." When we apply this term to the Adventist Christian world, we might say that 99 percent are not "especially skilled" Christians, in the sense that they are not trained pastors.

Tragically, this demeans Christians who are skilled in the spiritual gifts other than professional pastoring, as listed in 1 Corinthians 12 and Ephesians 4. The term *laity* judges all other spiritual gifts by the pastoral leadership gift alone, and judges all who bear these other gifts as lesser gift bearers. The words *just* and *layman* often end up in the same sentence.

In addition to the injustice this word serves, the term *laity* insults. When my dad, a physician, talks about some medical procedure, I say,

"Dad, explain that to me in layman's terms." I have no problem asking this, because when it comes to medicine, I am a layman. But what words should a pastor use? Should there be a professional vocabulary *and* a bone-head one?

The connotations of *lay* imply less-than-desirable notions. You know the old joke about lay activities on Sabbath—you plan to do nothing but sleep.

I see a major thrust in the church to increase the active ministry of Adventist members. I have heard this defined many times as "to increase lay involvement." Could it be that the term *lay* obstructs the intention of the phrase?

I believe a first step in more actively engaging all the spirit gifts of Adventists in church ministry is to view their gifts as equal to the pastoral gift. We must change some of our vocabulary to reach this goal.

I challenge Adventist churches, publications, pastors, medical work-ers, and evangelists, as well as musicians, administrators, teachers, com-forters, counselors, greeters, deacons, janitors, cooks, and the whole army of ministry, to declare "anathema" any reference to the word *laity*. We are all called as priests before God to minister to one another with our par-ticular spiritual gifts.

I challenge our church to ban both the word and the attitude behind it from pulpits and pages and pews. We must be not only politically cor-rect, but *biblically* correct.

"And to perseverance, godliness . . ."

GET OUT OF THE BARN
Victor Czerkasij

A stag found himself running for his life. Hounds and hunters followed in dogged pursuit. Where to hide? What to do? Spotting a barn at the far edge of a wide meadow, the deer leaped to its safety.

Skidding to a halt in front of the great open entrance, he bleated for help. "Brothers! Cousins!" he shouted to the cow and oxen. "Save me from certain death!"

Blinking in the sunlight, one bovine thoughtfully considered the situation. "If you hide in the corner stall and keep your antlers low, there's a chance you'll live." Shaking with relief, the stag did as he was told.

The hunting party arrived moments later. Confused by the myriad scents in the barnyard and urged on by the hunters, the dogs struck off down a trail, leaving the stag unharmed.

"Th-thank you," the stag stammered. "You saved my life."

Chewing with great satisfaction, the cow and oxen nodded to each other in their cleverness. "Stag, before you go," the cow said, "we have one question. Tell us, what is it like to live in the woods, beyond the pasture fence? What does it mean to be wild and free?" Flattered, the deer regaled the barn animals with every close encounter he had ever experienced and shared some extras he made up on the hoof.

The comfort of fresh straw, the cool shade of the barn, clean water and friendship with his newfound comrades, distracted the stately animal from returning to the forest.

Night arrived, bringing with it the dejected hunters and hounds returning from their chase. After kenneling the dogs and muttering about the day's defeat, the hunters ventured into the barn to attend to their small herd.

Imagine their surprise as they encountered the very object of the chase that day. Imagine the horror of the stag who had overstayed his visit.

The deer lost his life that night because he became comfortable in a place he should never have been complacent, a place he didn't belong.

Early in my teen years, after joining the Adventist Church, I vigorously nodded my head in response to the question "Do you want Jesus to return?" Of course I did. At that point I was staying close to the Lord. But as I spent less time with my God, I began to nod with less vigor and began qualifying my answers in my heart.

"Well, of course I want Jesus to return. Right after college graduation. Oh, and the honeymoon. And after the Cubs win the World Series."

These sentiments, safe in themselves, should never be placed in competition with *the* cosmic event of the universe. The Blessed Hope became the Fairly Important Hope as I gradually grew comfortable with living my life for myself.

I barely remember college graduation, because the family camera broke that day. True, I spent the honeymoon with the one I love, but after all these years it doesn't compare well with how much greater my marriage is *now*. And the Cubs? I really do want Jesus to come in my lifetime.

Johann Sebastian Bach chose to create and perform only one kind of music: that which glorifies God. Some thought he was limiting himself, but Bach had it right. By praising the Eternal, by lifting up the Perfect, he unwittingly created for himself a niche that to this day is referred to as *classic*. Hey, the name says it all.

MTV runs a program, so I'm told, that features one-hit wonders— bands with one song or video that rockets to the top and then you wonder what became of them. After 350 years Bach is still going strong because he did not limit his thinking to the present and temporal.

In eastern Pennsylvania on a gray day in November 1863, Edward Everett spoke before a crowd for two hours. After Everett finished, Abraham Lincoln spoke for less than two minutes there at Gettysburg and secured his place in history by lifting the twin virtues of freedom and unity.

One hundred years later, speaking at the nation's capital, Martin Luther King, Jr., shared his dream embraced by and entwined with Scripture. "I Have a Dream" was no spiritual monopoly held by one dreamer. All who heard King's words caught the dream.

Though Lincoln and King are gone, they live on through what they held dear in life. Their influence lives on because of what they sought for and treasured on this earth.

It would have been easy for Lincoln to rant against the Southerners and promise to crush them like ants. It would have been far simpler for King to ask for complacency and live with the times. With no vision, with no godliness, what else could have happened?

To me, the Sermon on the Mount is the most powerful discourse ever spoken to human ears, simply because Jesus was not willing to be a flatterer or a wit. He didn't care about being fashionable or steeped in conventional wisdom. He wanted to be right. His greatness arose from His godliness.

We are not called to mimic old platitudes. We are called to be Seventh-day Adventist Christians. We are called to godliness. Not to equal God in His awesome power and omniscience, but to reflect His character.

"For all who are being led by the Spirit of God, these are sons of God. For you have not received a spirit of slavery leading to fear again, but you have received a spirit of adoption as sons by which we cry out 'Abba! Father!'" (Romans 8:14, 15, NASB).

Listen. You don't belong in the barn of this world. You were not supposed to get comfortable in it. You are neither a cow nor an ox, but a child of God. Come out into the sun.

"And to godliness, brotherly kindness . . ."

AN OLD RECIPE FOR CHANGE
Andy Nash

*I*t's no secret. One of the most powerful things we can do is accept someone who doesn't expect to be accepted. It's no secret that when we do this—when we give someone a second chance—*everything changes*. It's no secret, because we've seen everything change before.

When Esau accepted a scheming brother who had conned him out of his birthright, *everything changed* (see Genesis 33).

When Joseph accepted 10 scheming brothers who had sold him into slavery, *everything changed* (see Genesis 45).

When Hosea accepted a wife who had cheated on him repeatedly, *everything changed* (see Hosea 1-3).

When Jesus accepted children who interrupted Him (see Mark 10:13-16); a Samaritan who argued with Him (see John 4:1-42); an adulterous woman who was thrown at Him (see John 8:1-11); a short tax collector who might have cheated Him (see Luke 19:1-9); a pair of blind beggars who shouted at Him (see Matthew 20:29-34); a best friend who deserted Him (see Matthew 26:69-75; John 21:15-19); a mob that murdered Him (see Luke 23:34); and a world that deserves to be condemned by Him (see John 3:17), *everything changed*.

So it's no secret that when we, as a church and as individuals, accept the "unacceptable"—

- seventh graders who look weird and act weirder;
- academy kids who smoke and swear;
- women who wear jewelry;
- men who wear jewelry;
- radicals who want drums in church;
- traditionalists who insist on the organ;
- those in favor of women's ordination and those who have a fit about it;
- those who have lost their regular standing;
- those who never had it;

- those who have hurt us before and those who would hurt us again;
- those who mock the true Sabbath;
- those who say sinners burn in hell;
- Mormons, Catholics, *Davidians*—

when it dawns on us that we *all* have different struggles because we're all different people, and that most people are just doing about the best they can, when we accept others as Jesus accepts us, *everything will change.*

Probably more than we can imagine.

"And to godliness, brotherly kindness . . ."

NERO CHECKED UNDER HIS BED
Victor Czerkasij

*G*rowing up with a brother two years younger, I didn't always consider him as someone to appreciate so much as someone to torture. The fact that he was bigger than I was made the whole scenario dangerously attractive.

If, from under the bed, I grab his legs, he'll have me cornered like a rat and pummel me to death, I'd reason. *But he'll also turn white as snow and shriek like a hyena.* So, after weighing the benefits of seeing Jerry near death against the drawback of finding myself in the same condition a minute later, I'd crawl under his bed and wait.

Needless to say, he never told me he loved me.

After school one day my underappreciated humor found me surrounded by a group of public school classmates. I was getting the short end of the stick and the pain factor was headed for warp drive, when a pudgy little kid yelled, "Leave my brother alone!" and began biting like a lion in the Serengeti.

It was Jerry. In an instant everyone let me go and turned on him. As his flesh and blood and older mentor, I mentally thanked him and ran like the gutless wonder I was.

When he got home, he looked as nonchalant as a person with blood and torn clothing can muster. What he had done, coupled with a casual "Anytime you need help, let me know," helped me to see him in a new light.

Jerry was always kind to me. But in this situation his benevolence showed up clearly in contrast to my unkindness and the fury of the crowd. It took a personal encounter with evil to show me what I had overlooked in my brother all along.

The work of someone like Mother Teresa seems the more significant because we see it against the backdrop of unimaginable horror, cruelty, and degradation. The gulf between good and evil seems so enormous that we marvel that either can exist in the other's presence. Brotherly kindness seems more remarkable in the face of brotherly hate.

THE RIDE OF YOUR LIFE

My parents grew up in unusual circumstances. Early in life they found World War II on their doorstep. As a young girl, my mom was forced to watch her parents being humiliated by camp guards, who took perverse pleasure in torture and mental anguish. The prisoners had nicknamed one of these demons in the flesh "Nero." The name seemed to fit in every way.

Nero did not realize for a while that he was a marked man. But with the war nearing its close, the American troops were liberating the camps one by one. They usually left justice to the inmates, who found the reversal of roles an answer to prayer. About this time Nero himself found prayer.

After liberation the inmates at my mom's camp discovered Nero trying to disguise himself as a woman. The group decided that his execution should be accomplished by drawing lots. After all, who wouldn't give in to the joy of personally putting to death someone who had murdered so many?

The lot fell to a 14-year-old girl, who promptly slit Nero from ear to ear as men held down the hated ex-camp guard. They dumped Nero into a nearby stream, where his boots stuck out and hundreds lined up to spit their mouths dry at this friendless soul.

Mom arrived at the camp just after the deed was done. She had been brought back after trying to escape west. The Americans wanted her to take part in the repatriation process.

The young girl who had killed Nero was one of Mom's close friends, and she was ecstatic to share her story. "Alla!" she squealed. "I got to kill Nero, and you missed it!" Mom replied that it was a low point in her life to have missed a glorious opportunity like that.

Years later, when I was a boy of 5 or 6, I remember a very old woman coming to our house once in a while. Mom would give her a meal and fill her dirty plastic bags with food and clothing. The woman never spoke. The unkempt hair, the tattered clothing, the wizened face and clouded eyes, put fear into me. Mom would hold her and sing songs about heartache and lost love, which is pretty much standard fare in Ukrainian music.

Mom didn't tell us who the woman was until years later.

"Do you remember the girl who killed Nero? That lady who came to the house was the same girl."

Incredulous, I protested that she was too different to be the same age as my mother. And, I reminded Mom, she had said in the past that the 14-year-old girl was as pretty as a model. I had seen a classic bag lady come to our house.

Mom's eyes grew serious. "No one who murders can ever hope to escape from what they inflict, no matter how just the cause or how deep the pain. She snapped soon after she killed Nero, and only America would take her in."

When Jesus Christ walked on the earth, He exemplified perfection. Not a harsh word or a glance of hate for all the injustices He suffered. Only acts of compassion, patience, and kindness. Even more mind-boggling, His kindness followed the greatest concentrated effort of evil ever produced. Yet He did not flirt with the dark side, nor ever desired to. His kindness shone bright against the canvas of hatred all around. How did He do it?

Do you remember what Peter adds to perseverance? Godliness. Once God places the desire for godliness into your heart, brotherly kindness always follows.

Kindness does not come naturally to us. We are selfish from the womb and want the very biggest and best piece from day one. This puts us in conflict with each other because we share the same selfish goal.

When we give ourselves up to God, He shows us how to grow into Christ's character. He replaces our selfish desires with selfless ones. We become willing to hand away the biggest and best. Godliness takes hold.

My favorite TV program is *America's Funniest Home Videos*. One episode features my friend Andy Nash as a boxer who knocks the lights out of a chandelier. (He got a T-shirt out of the deal.) The show receives top ratings because it shows people falling out of trees, being run over by bulls, losing control of their empty cars over cliffs, and other comical mishaps caught on camera. I find myself playing every pie-in-the-face in glorious slo-mo. (Ha! Ha! Look at that chandelier fall!)

I would feel absolutely wretched if any of these things happened to me. But the brotherly kindness God wishes for us requires that we picture ourselves in the other person's shoes in *every* situation. God wants us to see other people as He sees them and to love them as He does, with no thought of reward. ("Boy, those lights falling on your head must have really hurt.")

"For if we died with Him, we shall also live with Him; if we endure, we shall also reign with Him; if we deny Him, He also will deny us; if we are faithless, He remains faithful" (2 Timothy 2:11-13, NASB).

Jerry and I talked this evening. I had heard that most of California was being declared a disaster area for some reason, and I called to check on him.

"We're fine," he said. "Nothing for you to worry about. And, Victor, I appreciate you calling. You know I love you."

I know he does. His wife says he never checks under the bed anymore.

"And to godliness, brotherly kindness . . ."

LIVE A LITTLE
Andy Nash

You may have heard the story.

A man sets out to save as many starfish as he can. Early each morning he combs the beach where he lives, searching for starfish to save. When he finds one, he slings it as far as he can into the sea. Then he looks for more.

One morning a beach stroller sees the man hunting for starfish and flinging them into the sea.

"Excuse me," the beach stroller says to the man. "Why are you throwing starfish into the sea?"

"I have decided that I'm going to save all the beached starfish in the world," the man replies.

"That's ridiculous!" says the beach stroller. "There must be millions and millions of starfish lying on the world's beaches. You can't possibly make a difference."

"I suppose you're right," the man says as he digs up another starfish and slings it into the sea. "But I can make a difference to *that* one."

The man had made a difference to many starfish, perhaps thousands. *Was his starfish mission successful?* You can argue that question either way.

In one sense the man's starfish mission succeeded because starfish, quite simply, were being saved. The man certainly had the right attitude: He saw each starfish as important in itself. Saving even one doomed starfish made the mission a success.

At the same time, though, the starfish mission was not as successful as it could be. Though one man achieved a difference in the lives of *some* starfish, he couldn't possibly reach even a small fraction of the starfish beached around the world. The beach stroller sized up the situation accurately: One person can't save millions of starfish.

I find the world mission of our church in similar shape. *Is our world mission successful?* Yes, it is. And no, it isn't.

On one hand, we can rate our world mission a success because people are being brought to the Lord. If you could fly around the world right now, you would

- see Adventist English teachers in language schools invite their students to stick around for free Bible classes, and watch students stick around;
- see Adventist camp nurses patch up refugees, and hear many of those refugees ask about the God the nurses say they work for;
- hear Adventist evangelists and their interpreters present the gospel to people in Russia and Mongolia, Guatemala and Brazil;
- see Adventist professionals in secular overseas posts (we call them "tentmakers"), hear them slip the name of Jesus into their professional conversations, and watch non-Adventist professionals responding to the name of Jesus.

So to say that this church's world mission is not a success would cheapen thousands of redeeming moments around the world.

On the other hand, to say that we couldn't do much, much better would be just as inappropriate. We may be impressed by the report that we've "reached" 209 of 236 countries and 3,000 of 5,257 ethnolinguistic groups in the world. But too often, "reached" means that we've placed one church among millions of people. That's not reached—that's pinpricked. By suggesting that Global Mission is a smashing success, we deter the urgency of mission among our people. That's all we need—a bunch of American Adventists thinking we've just about covered the whole world.

The bottom line is that in this world one in every 750 people is an Adventist. We need to do better than that before we deem Global Mission a success, before we talk about turning foreign missions over to indigenous peoples. The needs are great and will remain great until we paint an accurate picture of our mission accomplishments (possibly by comparing ourselves with other, more successful mission groups), and sound the alarm once more.

And that's where we come in.

No one—*no one*—in this church is in a better position to reach the world than young Adventists. Why? Because, unlike our elders, many of us don't have big families, houses, cars, and long-term job commitments—all of which tend to lock people into a life here in America. We do have the energy, enthusiasm, flexibility, and open-mindedness needed in foreign missions.

Of course, many young Adventists have already gone out to meet the need. Each year hundreds of student missionaries and a handful of young graduates fly out of American airports for a year or two of overseas service. But there aren't enough of them; there aren't enough of *us*. We no longer see mission as a must but as a maybe.

One hundred years ago Ellen Write wrote that our church schools should prepare workers in the shortest time possible, that they may go out with the message. But today our schools seem to focus more on making it in the world than saving the world.

A friend of mine, Steve Nyirady, spent his twenty-first year as a refugee-camp nurse on the Thailand-Burma border and plans to go back. He suggests that many of us see mission as merely another option—a neat way to spend a year. "But," Steve says, "mission isn't an option. Realizing that Jesus Christ saved you—you can't keep that message to yourself. If you don't share that message, you're shirking your responsibility as a Christian."

"OK, fair enough," say some. "But do you have to go overseas to be a missionary? After all, America is a mission field too, right?"

Right. America *is* a mission field. Our "Christian" nation still needs Christ. From rescuing teenagers in inner-city Philadelphia to feeding migrant workers living in barns in Oregon, we can find plenty to do in America. *So spend 78 of your 80 years sharing God's love with Americans.*

But how about a year or two where you're *really* needed—with a people who don't hear the name of Jesus every time they flip through the TV channels, in a country without a church on every street corner? How about a little help where it's *desperately* needed—in Buddhist lands, in Hindu lands, in Muslim lands? How about catching the spirit of Paul and Peter, who could have stayed home but didn't? How about calling the church mission number (1-800-331-2767) and checking out your options? How about it?

Live a little. You're young only once.

"'I tell you the truth,' Jesus replied, 'no one who has left home or brothers or sisters or mother or father or children or fields for me and the gospel will fail to receive a hundred times as much in this present age . . . and in the age to come, eternal life'" (Mark 10:29, 30, NIV).

"And to godliness, brotherly kindness . . ."

THE THEOLOGY OF SISTER MARY CLARENCE (AKA WHOOPI GOLDBERG)

Alex Bryan

Church \ 'cherch \ *n* 1: a place good law-abiding citizens go once a week (see *Little House on the Prairie*) 2: a habit; much like brushing teeth, buying groceries, getting one's hair cut 3: a duty; similar to voting for president and donating to charity 4: a way to please one's parents 5: a place to meet girls 6: the preamble to Sabbath lunch and nap 7: the occasion I iron pants, wear coat and tie, tell everybody how perfect my life is.

What is your definition of church? Perhaps it is a conglomeration of many definitions. Mine is. And *how* it has changed over the years.

What if I told you, "I *love* the church"? You might turn to the next chapter. "He's one of them. He learned those memory verses in kindergarten. He always went up front. He longed for *Ingathering*. He sang out really loud in youth Sabbath school. He grew up pumped up about the church. He can't be trusted!"

So what if I learned memory verses in kindergarten? You probably did too. I got up front now and then, *Ingathered* cash for the poor in poor neighborhoods (go figure), and sang out on "Do Lord." But that was about it. Church was a way of life, not an event to get excited about.

Let's face it: for most, *church* is not one of those words that quickens the heart rate and stimulates the salivary glands. *Super Bowl. Spring break. Baskin-Robbins ice cream.* These are the real high points in life. Have you ever lain awake Friday night, anticipating church the next morning? Have you ever lain awake Saturday night (or early Sunday morning) reflecting on your church experience?

I never could sleep the night before the first day of school; nor before my family vacation to the beach; nor before the arrival of my West Coast cousins; and not the night before Christmas. I still can't sleep the night after another amazing Atlanta Braves' come-from-behind victory; after a long-distance conversation with a good friend; and the night after Christmas. I stay excited about these memorable experiences. Unlike my feelings for church.

But should church be memorable in the same way?

I would say yes, if we choose *Little House* as our model and define church as just another stop on the assembly line of human existence and nothing more.

But we'd have to answer no if the New Testament and *Sister Act* define what the church should be. Call it theology according to the apostle Luke and Whoopi Goldberg.

In the film *Sister Act* a nun named Sister Mary Clarence (played by Whoopi Goldberg) is actually no woman of God. She is a woman of the world in a witness protection program, disguised as a nun. She finds herself assigned to an out-of-touch church in New York City with meager attendance and boring services—far from memorable.

Sister Mary Clarence can't believe a church could be so irrelevant. She decides to change things. She takes over the choir, and the music evolves from mundane to toe-tapping. She encourages the other nuns to engage "sinners" in the community. She leads a cleanup campaign, turning the dark, uninviting church into an attraction for visitors. She organizes a yard sale to benefit the needy. And what happens? Attendance rises exponentially, dreary pew-sitting becomes exuberant worship, burned-out nuns experience real revival, and the pope himself pays a visit.

What makes the difference? Sister Mary Clarence convinces the church to trade in a wall for a welcome mat. A church that said *"Go away!"* now says *"Come on in!"*

Lest you doubt the theology of *Sister Act*, read Jesus' stories in Luke's Gospel:

"The master told his servant, 'Go out to the roads and country lanes and make them come in, so that my house will be full'" (Luke 14:23, NIV).

Read about the tax collectors and "sinners" who gathered around to hear Him. And hear the Pharisees and the teachers of the law muttering, "This fellow welcomes sinners and eats with them" (Luke 15:2, NIV).

Jesus told the people these parables to show His purpose: a shepherd goes after a lost sheep; a woman searches for a lost coin; a father watches for a lost son. "We had to celebrate and be glad," the father says to the son who's not lost, "because this brother of yours was dead and is alive again; he was lost and is found" (verse 32, NIV).

Jesus talks about what makes the church a great place to be. He says it should be filled with fishers of men (see Matthew 4:19). It has a Great Commission to baptize disciples in all the world (see Matthew 28:19, 20). It's a hospital in which He, the Physician, will cure the sick (see Matthew 9:12). Repeatedly, He tells us what it means to be a Christian and why it makes life in His church so thrilling.

For years I played around with the *Little House* definition of church—a club for saints. And how boring it was. Now I know that church represents something entirely different: a house of salvation. Jesus, with a little help from Whoopi Goldberg, showed me how. I learned to focus on *them* instead of *us*. *Them* sinners, you might say.

On this earth Jesus grew up in a church completely focused on itself. Jewish synagogues said, "Go away!" Sinners felt discouraged from going anywhere near the church. The insiders made sure the outsiders never got in. Insiders who showed signs of becoming like the outsiders were booted out before they polluted the holy atmosphere. At best the church of Jesus' time was very dull; at worst, frightful.

Jesus expressed displeasure with the state of the church. He knew it must change or fall further into irrelevance. So He started a revolution to remake His church. It would no longer focus on the current members, but would turn its attention to the salvation needs of sinners. It would be a place to fish, baptize, and cure the masses.

His plan caught fire and swept across the Mediterranean world. It shocked the contemporary culture and disrupted an empire. Long after His death (which came as a result of His new church ideas) the revolution continued. Revolutionaries (called Christians) lost their friends, families, and fortunes in the name of their new cause. Many were tortured and killed for their new beliefs. And church was no longer dull.

Intentionally making church a life-threatening experience probably should not be our approach to reviving a sleeping church. One day it may happen, but there's no sense risking lives just to stir things up a bit. Martyrdom was not what made the early Christian church so exciting anyway. The thrill factor was selling God—for free.

I'll guarantee you something: *If you convince your church to focus entirely on marketing God to a world desperately seeking Him, you will find church life the most exciting and rewarding part of your life.* Believe it or not, you may even lie awake at night thinking about it.

Start by getting to know unchurched people. You don't have to slam the beasts of Revelation down their throat, either. Just befriend them: go golfing, play tennis, join a health club, hit the mall together, take in a concert or a ballgame. Before you know it, you'll be caring about lost people. Once you care about lost people, funny things will start to happen. You may notice for the first time that your church does not offer a safe environment in which to place unchurched friends. Will the lawn be mowed? Do we keep the church clean? Will the bulletin speak English or Adventese? Will the announcements go on forever? Will the music be in tune? Will the words mean *anything* to my non-Christian friend? Will someone beg for money? Will the prayer sound like normal speech? Will the sermon bore us? Will my visiting friend have to wear a big VISITOR sticker and stand up in front of a crowd he or she doesn't know? Will anyone care that my friend might be making an *eternal* decision this bright, sunny Sabbath morning?

Just imagine how church would change if *everyone* in your church began making friends for God and inviting them in. The stale routine would give way to a heaven event framed in the four walls of your church.

Your spiritual indicators would change too: prayer life, financial priorities, time commitment. They would go up. Church discipline, petty fights, Christological controversy—all would go down. A full-fledged assault on Satan's influence would awaken our spiritual energies.

Adventist churches across North America are beginning to discover the spiritual freshness of a *them-focused* church. They have experienced some growth and a renewed commitment to God and each other. They see lifeless churches transforming into centers for life-giving Christian experience.

If *you* start putting gospel principles to work, your church life will become very exciting. Taste one or two conversions, and the fever will get in you. Participate in bringing the lost to Jesus and experience the most thrilling thing under creation. Your skepticism of "church lovers" like me will die out, and you will develop your own love for the church you call home. The anticipation for Sabbath morning and the other six days you're involved in church life will become infectious.

What's your definition of church? You must decide.

"And to brotherly kindness, love."

MY GIRL
Andy Nash

"Who is this that appears like the dawn, fair as the moon, bright as the sun, majestic as the stars in procession?" (Song of Solomon 6:10, NIV).

ast summer I married the girl I had always dreamed about marrying. The one I knew was out there somewhere. The one I thought I'd never find. Her name, as you know by now, is Cindy.

Cindy and I met at a college cafeteria table. She mostly ignored me. I mostly ignored her back. After two weeks of mutual ignoring, I felt that our relationship was ready for the next step—no, not miniature golf, but talking.

I resolved to call her room in Thatcher Hall. But I felt nervous. Real nervous. The kind of nervous a seventh-grader feels when he's about to call a girl for the first time. To call Cindy across campus, all I had to do was dial four digits—2259—but I just could not get past the 5: 2-2-5-*click*, 2-2-5-*click*. So instead, I sat on my bed and wrung my hands and wondered what it would be like to press the 9.

Then, with a sudden burst of courage I pressed all four numbers.

Then I stammered four words. "Cindy? This is Andy."

Then I asked her for a date.

Later I asked her for another.

Then she asked *me* for another.

Then I asked her for a kiss.

Then she asked me for some time.

Then I knew for whom I'd waited.

Then I asked him for her hand.

Then I promised her, "Forever."

Falling in love. Can you describe it? I can't. I used to smirk at my whipped friends when they fell hard for a girl.

"You're pathetic," I would tell them. "Snap out of it." After I met Cindy, people began telling *me* to snap out of it. I never did.

THE RIDE OF YOUR LIFE

Yes, I know that many people say love is more than a feeling—it's a decision, they insist. Fine, fine. Let the debate rage. All I know is that I love Cindy because I'm happy when she's around and because I miss her when she isn't.

When Cindy's around, I'm happy. I love her shining blue eyes, her soft hands, and her smile. I love knowing I'm at least partially responsible for that smile. I love the way she pulls her long, dark hair up on each side and clips it with that gold thing on top—because she knows I like it that way. I love how she looks in her emerald-green overcoat (stunning) when we go to church. I love how she walks. I love how she laughs. I love how she holds little children and hugs old people. I love how she insists O.J. is innocent. I love how she cries at anything sad, even at TV commercials, and how she gets embarrassed that she's crying at a commercial and how she elbows me for laughing at her. I love how, when I take her golfing, she tries to use a tee on the fairway. I love how she asks me questions that I don't have a chance to answer: "And, Andy, I want to get a new sundress, do you know why? Because then I can wear it spring break, that's why." I love how she made plans day and night for our wedding. And mostly I love how she wants to spend the rest of her days with me.

Days come, of course, when Cindy and I can't spend time together. But that doesn't mean my love for her diminishes; if anything, it increases. Last spring, for example, my scuba-diving class traveled to Florida for our checkout dive. Cindy stayed in Tennessee. I enjoyed the dive, and the view underwater was fascinating, but all I could think about was how I wished Cindy could be there with me.

After our dive, I did something I simply never do. I sat down and wrote a poem. I wrote about how much I wished Cindy could have witnessed all the marine life and the colors with me. The poem was entitled "I Saw a Manatee Today, and I Thought of You." I gave it to Cindy when I returned, but she didn't seem to like it as much as I had hoped she would.

Failed poems aside, you get the idea. I'm happy when Cindy's around, and I miss her when she isn't. And that's why I'm in love with her.

But that's not why I married her.

I married her because of something much deeper and much more secure than how happy I feel when I'm around Cindy. I married her because she loves the same God and the same church I do.

Of course, Cindy's membership in the Adventist Church wasn't the original reason I took an interest in her. Guys aren't attracted to girls just because they're Adventist.

"Hey, bud. Check ooouuuut that girl. She looks Adventist."

"Yeah, I see what you mean. Man, she's looking very Adventist today."

"You can say that again."

Adventists fall in love for the same reasons non-Adventists do: looks, personality, and character. We don't choose whom we fall in love with. (If you don't think so, then put yourself in a non-Adventist setting for a year and see how well you take an interest in nobody.) That's why the right dating environment is so important. The way I see it, going to an Adventist college or an Adventist singles weekend doesn't guarantee falling in love with a suitable mate, but it sure increases the odds. It did for me.

Still, some may ask, "Why does it matter whether or not we marry someone who holds similar beliefs?"

The answer is simple: Because God says so. *"Can two walk together, except they be agreed?"* (Amos 3:3, KJV). In His perfect foresight and wisdom, God knew that marriage would be complicated enough without having to work out differences in church, lifestyle, behavior standards, and goals.

I believe God intended marriage to be permanent—both in Eden and now. Why would He encourage His children to mix the happiness of marriage with uncertainties about how long that happiness would last? And why in the world would He use the bride/bridegroom metaphor for Christ and the church if marriage were not intended to last throughout life?

But if we expect God to honor His side of the agreement, to inspire a happy marriage, then we must honor ours and marry a believer. If we don't, we have no assurance of anything. Samson can vouch for that.

Do not marry someone who believes differently than you, says the Lord. How can you, who believes in Me, be married to someone who doesn't believe in Me? You can't be partners with an unbeliever. No more than Jesus can team up with Satan. No more than a creationist can agree with an evolutionist.

Instead, says the Lord, if you are an Adventist and serious about it, please be serious about the biggest decision of your life. Please marry another who believes as you do. If you do, I will be with both of you in a very special way, as I promise to be when two or three are gathered in My name. If you do, I will pour out My blessings upon your marriage. And if you do, I will call you My children (see 2 Corinthians 6:14-18; Matthew 18:20).

And so, with that promise and without reservation, Cindy and I began our lives together on June 25, 1995. The statistics we all hear about? We're not going to worry about them. The Bible gives us a formula for happiness and for serving our Creator together, and we're going to follow it the best we can. The blessings we're leaving to the Lord. And the poetry I'm leaving to the poets.

> *"Place me like a seal over your heart, like a seal on your arm; for love is as strong as death, its jealousy unyielding as the grave. It burns like blazing fire, like a mighty flame" (Song of Solomon 8:6, NIV).*

"And to brotherly kindness, love."

My Hero
Alex Bryan

"I have come that they may have life, and have it to the full" (John 10:10, NIV).

Heroes are hard to come by in this world. The popularity of Superman, Michael Jordan, Tom Clancy's Jack Ryan, and a host of other film, sport, and fictional book heroes illustrates how life is short on champions. If we can't find them in the *real* world, at least we can play make-believe.

I am fortunate to have found a real-life hero. My hero did not wear a capital *S* on his chest, dunk basketballs with amazing artistry, or save the world from nuclear war in less than 800 pages. He is a hero of greater consequence—a hero sent by God. In His goodness, God delivered a real-life superhero in my path. With divine grace, God gave me Tim Kroll.

I knew Tim since he was 6 until he died at 25 last spring. We grew up together, from little boys discussing baseball and playing Monopoly to grown men discussing world events and playing Monopoly. But Tim was more than *my* friend and hero, to be sure. Many discovered an unforgettable influence he had on their lives. Here's why.

Tim not only defied the law that heroes do not exist, he destroyed several other standbys in a sin-plagued world. He suffered from muscular dystrophy, a terminal disease that weakens the muscles of the body. As a young boy Tim was increasingly hindered by his disease; as a man it put him in a wheelchair and took away his freedom to eat, read, and write without assistance. His friends drove Tim in a special van for the physically impaired. They opened doors and carried books for him. Tim was totally dependent on others to help carry out his daily functions of life. Muscular dystrophy, which afflicted and eventually ended his life, tragically demonstrated the way Satan governs.

Tim, meanwhile, valiantly demonstrated the way God will govern for eternity. In a fallen world, Tim embodied the world to come.

THE RIDE OF YOUR LIFE

Even in the face of incomprehensible difficulty he brought comfort to others. On a trip to Gatlinburg, Tennessee, his family and mine embarked on a hike through the beauty of the Smoky Mountains. We picked a large trail so Tim could come along in his wheelchair. His two brothers, my two brothers, and I would take turns pushing him along the path. As an ambitious little boy, I decided it would be fun to get far ahead of the rest and so, pushing Tim in front of me, I made every effort to increase the margin of our lead. Minutes later we were well ahead of the pack. About every 30 or 40 feet a log lay diagonally across the path. Half-embedded in the ground, these logs were designed to provided drainage for the trail. Every so often, a log would present a minimal challenge for Tim and me. But simply aligning the large rear wheels of the chair with the log enabled us to easily overcome the barrier. I carefully tilted the chair backward and placed the small front wheels up and over each log. With caution this was no problem.

But *caution* is not of first importance in moving *rapidly* along a trail. Speed is. And this became a problem. I pulled Tim's wheelchair up over a log—one wheel *before* the other—and instantly I knew we were in trouble. The chair flipped over. Unable to break his rapid descent, Tim fell hard to the ground. My heart raced. What was I going to do? I couldn't lift him. I yelled back for help until his parents and mine picked up his scratched and bleeding body and put him back in his wheelchair.

I have never hurt so much inside.

Tim wasn't thrilled he had been dumped so hard and carelessly onto the ground. But never did he scold me, yell at me, or deny me the privilege of pushing him again. For Tim, forgiveness was second nature, and forgetting was certain.

I wish dumping Tim out of his wheelchair as a child were the only time I treated Tim inadequately. Many times my friends and I would play basketball for hours, leaving Tim to sit in his chair and watch TV or read a book. Often I was not as quick as I should have been to assist in a basic need he was unable to perform for himself. A simple task like adjusting his glasses, getting him a drink, bringing him another book to read, or taking him for a drive in his custom-designed van were usually his request rather than my offer. He asked for my help far less than he should, and I asked to help him far less than I should. But Tim always forgave, always forgot, and always greeted me with a smile or some timely humor. Despite my faults, Tim's friendship remained constant.

Perhaps most striking about Tim was the incredible magnetism he generated for those left out of the cliques in society. He always had time to take a phone call, a visit, or a *really* long visit from someone in need of listening ears. Tim's Jesus-like sensitivity toward human need took much of his time—time others would spend on themselves. It wasn't that *Tim* demanded the time of others. His popularity exceeded that of every academy and college student during his years in Adventist education. His time was God's time, and "Unto the least of these my brethren" marked the life of my hero.

Tim's magical quality did not come from his disease, however. What made him rare was his powerful insight on what is important and what is not in life.

He knew what was important. Tim studied hard. Though it was difficult for him to take notes in class, maneuver large textbooks, and research in the library, he knew far more than any of us. When conversations on world trivia, history, or current events came up, we became his students and he our teacher. Tim's interest in history spread to politics. In 1988 he met Barbara Bush. In October 1992 he shook the hand of President George Bush. He also kept abreast of news in the Adventist Church—from the GC to SC. His involvement in the student association at Southern College provided an avenue for service to many students. Most of all, he spent time with his friends, called his family often, and always worshiped God on Sabbath. No book sat on his desk—opened—more than the Bible. When I entered his room down the hall in our college dormitory he often would ask me to take a book off his shelf and place it on his wheelchair desk. Sometimes it was *Sports Illustrated*, sometimes it was one of many thick history books, but mostly it was the leather-bound pages that directed his life.

Tim knew what wasn't important, too. For starters, radical health habits. He loved Mexican cuisine and put away burritos with amazing veracity. He also knew too much study was harmful. North Carolina basketball *always* drew Tim's attention—and a crowd in his room—to root on his favorite team. He even met coach Dean Smith of the Tarheels. Their picture graced his wall. He knew how to treat a girl like a gentleman should and dated with grace and class. Like Jesus, he knew how to have fun. Rook games, excursions to the mall, late-night discussions, concerts, plays, and sporting events—his life was balanced like every Christian's should be.

I cannot understand what it is like to face the challenges he faced. As if his muscular dystrophy were not enough, his mother died just weeks before his academy graduation. Weeks later he would undergo major surgery. None other than Satan himself tried to shake the faith of this giant of God with most painful blows. Tim endured the cruelest hardships without rejecting a God who allowed the devil his way for a time.

The crowning triumph of his life came in the event of his college graduation. As class president, he symbolically led those who had followed him for many years. In his speech, which brought tears and comfort to the thousands of listeners, Tim emphasized the absolute assurance of God's salvation. "Today we should not say 'Goodbye,' but 'See you later,' because we know there is another time and another place waiting for us," he said. Tim cited the powerful words in Jeremiah 29:11: "'For I know the plans that I have for you,' declares the Lord, 'plans to prosper you and not to harm you, plans to give you hope and a future.'" His words brought a standing ovation—matched only by the ovation he later received as he drove across the platform to receive his diploma.

Tim is my hero. He is because he showed me clearly what my life should be. He exemplified the principles of Christ: love first for others, absolute faith in God, and a willingness to develop the character of God in his life. Tim died with an undaunted faith that he would be in heaven forever with his Best Friend. I want to live with such confidence. He knew how to conquer Satan. I want to deal with tragedy as successfully.

I opened this chapter with Jesus' words: "I have come that they may have life, and have it abundantly." Tim knew what living the abundant life was all about. It's about living with Jesus and everything else coming after that. Jesus is it. Period. His love filling my life abundantly. Because Tim accepted that love, he will enjoy the abundance of heaven forever.

Tim's prophetic call rings clear: "Not goodbye, but see you later." He knew his destiny, for he lived his hope. The question for you and me: Will we follow the example of my hero and accept the call to see him and *Him* one day? Will it be goodbye or see you later?

Tim's graduation speech proverb, "Do not measure your success in terms of today and tomorrow, but in eternity," is some pretty solid advice for young Adventists entering the adult world. Make no mistake: We constantly measure ourselves. Are we successful? Is this a good thing? Will this make me happy? How much will it add to my life? How far can I go in life? How much can I make? How good are my relationships?

In everything, *eternity* must be the standard. The abundant life is premised on eternal values. They help us sort out what's important and what isn't. We have touched on many of these values in this book. But most important is a love for God that is eternal. It's the kind of love that puts all else in perspective. It's the kind of love that gives real quality to life. It's the kind of love that hopes for eternity. These were Tim's values—learned in the pages of Scripture. Jesus longs for *us* to take on these values, too, and enjoy an abundance of life *in Him* forever.

Hero, I'll see you later. We'll go for a walk together . . . in the kingdom.

"And to brotherly kindness, love."

My God
Victor Czerkasij

My oldest son loves me. There are two ways I know this. First, he loves to spend every waking moment of his day with me. (Sometimes his waking moments begin well in advance of mine.) Second, I know that Alex loves me because nothing seems to break his heart more, after he's hurt his daddy, than to hear me say "Daddy is very sad." The tyke puts his lower lip up against his nostrils, squints his eyes, and gets ready for a good cry.

I like that. Not because it makes Alex cry, but because he hurts most when he knows he's hurt me. At 2 years old the kid knows the whole purpose of obedience. He knows what should motivate him to do right: He loves his father so much that he avoids doing anything that harms the relationship. And because he loves me, he looks for things to do that will make me laugh or respond with affection.

When Paul approached the early Christian church at Corinth, he found a host of problems: immorality, conceit, doctrinal confusion, and factions splitting the people into followers of either Paul, Apollos, Cephas, or Christ (see 1 Corinthians 1:12). He was so discouraged he even wrote that he was thankful he didn't have a hand in baptizing any of them except Crispus, Gaius, and the household of Stephanas, in order to protect his own name! What does one do when the prospects seem so bleak and the work so daunting?

Paul did the only thing he could do: He lifted the cross of Christ.

"When I came to you, brethren, I did not come with superiority of speech or of wisdom, proclaiming to you the testimony of God. For I am determined to know nothing among you except Jesus Christ, and Him crucified" (1 Corinthians 2:1, 2, NASB).

Why did Paul make the cross his rallying cry with the Corinthians? *Because nothing else would work.* How could pure love be better demonstrated than by the sacrifice of Jesus for a lost people?

The Greeks among them knew the fable in which Alcestis was willing to die for a good man named Admetus. They saw this as a tremendous display of affection. But notice that Alcestis was merely *willing*, and then only for a "worthy" individual.

Paul came along and told them the story of the one true God who did die on their behalf, and He went one better than the Greek goddess. He died for slaves, too—and temple prostitutes, gladiators, tax collectors, and an entire host of unsavory characters. Here was a God who loved mean, ugly, worthless people. Incredibly, His death gave them worth. This was what they had been waiting for.

Paul knew that lifting the cross alone would be successful. None could rely on self, and none could find glory in self. "I am a free man and owe no master," Paul said, "but I have made myself every man's servant, to win over as many as possible" (1 Corinthians 9:19, NEB).

The cross binds wounds and heals divisions. It's the center of every effort that Alex, Andy, and I have put forth. No reasoning or logic, no eloquent writing, will motivate you unless you receive Jesus completely into your life. No amount of Scripture, however pieced together, will bring a single doctrine to life if the Saviour isn't central.

Cab Calloway, an American entertainer for most of this century, wrote his epitaph just before he died in 1994. "Women, horses, cars, clothes. I did it all. And do you know what that's called, ladies and gentlemen? It's called living."

But clothes fade, cars rust, men and women and horses die. A life without God amounts to nothing.

Jesus Himself knew that in His mission on earth, He was to seek God first. He said to the people of His day, "How can you believe, when you receive glory from one another, and you do not seek the glory that is from the one and only God?" (John 5:44, NASB). But, He said, "He who sent Me is with Me; He has not left Me alone, *for I always do the things that are pleasing to Him*" (John 8:29, NASB). Jesus was completely energized by serving God and doing what pleased Him.

We don't seek God by a casual prayer or by thumbing through Scripture. We might think of Him as a family member lost in the woods. We would not shout His name a few times and, not hearing anything immediately, call it a night. We seek until we find.

John 12:42, 43 presents a searing indictment of what might have been if the people of Jesus' time had sought the Father. "Many even of the rulers believed in Him, but because of the Pharisees they were not confessing Him, lest they should be put out of the synagogue; for they loved the approval of men rather than the approval of God" (NASB).

Amazing! The people knew who Jesus was. Alas, the approval of their peers took precedence in their lives. Their own desires stopped them from saying with Paul, "I count all things but loss in view of the surpassing value of knowing Christ" (Philippians 4:8).

As a Bible teacher I would tell my students that in order for God to wipe away all tears, tears must be shed. We will shed them for those who knowingly pass by the gift of our God: Himself.

You might think that my son will outgrow his simple affection for his father one day. The cynic might say, "Yes, enjoy it while you can, because one day it won't matter much to him what a father thinks." Perhaps.

But love for the Father never dimmed for Jesus. Or Noah. Or Abraham, Isaac, Jacob, Daniel, Joseph, Caleb, Joshua, Isaiah, Ruth, and Jeremiah. Neither for Tyndale, Wycliffe, Luther. Or those who came out of their homes and barns on October 23, 1844. The approval of their heavenly Father was all that they ever wanted or needed, and it always exceeded their expectations.

George Mueller, the great builder of orphanages, once wrote, "There was a day when I died: I died to George Mueller: to his tastes, his opinions, his preferences, and his will. Died to the world—its approval or censure. Died to the approval or blame of brethren and friends. Since then I have studied only to show myself approved unto God." If only that were true of us all.

I must close now. Alex and Andy are waiting for this chapter to finish the book. Either that or they just love to hear my voice when they call every day. I hope we left you encouraged. I hope we sparked a renewed commitment to Him. I hope we touched your Adventist journey.

Until then, let this be sure: He will ever be our God, and we His children.

"For if you possess these qualities in increasing measure, they will keep you from being ineffective and unproductive in your knowledge of our Lord Jesus Christ."